Collins

need to know?

NLP

Carolyn Boyes

Collins

First published in 2006 by Collins
An imprint of
HarperCollins Publishers
77–85 Fulham Palace Road
London W6 8JB

www.collins.co.uk

10 09 08 07 06
6 5 4 3 2 1

A catalogue record for this book is available from
the British Library

Author: Carolyn Boyes
Editor: Elizabeth Hutchins
Designer: Bob Vickers
Series design: Mark Thomson
Illustrator: Ome Design
Front cover photograph: © Alamy Images
Back cover photographs: © Getty Images

ISBN-10 0-00-721655-6
ISBN-13 978-0-00-721655-0

Colour reproduction by Colourscan, Singapore
Printed and bound by Printing Express, Hong Kong

Important
The information (including without limitation advice and recommendations) contained
in this book is presented for general information purposes only and this book is
intended as a self-help aid. While extensive research has been carried out in the
preparation of this book, not all the information contained within will be suitable for
and/or helpful to all individuals. The author and HarperCollins assume no responsibility
for any consequence relating directly or indirectly to any action or inaction you take
based on the information, services or other material contained or implied in this book.
There is no implied endorsement of any product mentioned herein.

Contents

Introduction

Neuro-Linguistic Programming (NLP) is a way of thinking about how the world works. It is the study of excellence – and how you can achieve it. This book explains what Neuro-Linguistic Programming has to offer and how you can use it for success in your everyday life.

Why read this book?

Whatever you do for a living and whatever stage you are at in your life, whether young, middle aged or elderly, Neuro-Linguistic Programming can help you achieve more. If you are a business person, if you are in a relationship, if you want to improve a sport, get rid of a phobia, have greater satisfaction in your social life or change a habit, there are NLP techniques that you can use to create new results.

It may be that you would like to be a better communicator, have smoother relationships, greater career success, more money or just know yourself better. Perhaps you are very successful in conventional terms but there are still things you would like to change within yourself. NLP can show you how.

In your personal life, NLP can show you ways to create a personally fulfilling and happy life. In other words, you can use NLP to coach yourself. In business, you can use NLP to coach your colleagues, for sales, for presentations and for improved communication and management. You can also use NLP for personal coaching – for example, to help a person to get rid of a limiting belief or an unwanted habit, to refine his goals or to work with a series of issues.

How does NLP work?

NLP is concerned with how the top people in any area consistently achieve results. It is more than a way of thinking about success, though – it also provides a series of practical techniques that can be easily learned and applied to any area of life.

The belief that lies behind NLP is that each person who achieves outstanding results has a method, process and structure by which he does so. NLP analyses that person's thinking and behaviour to make a 'model' of excellence that anybody can use to replicate his success. Next, NLP takes this model and shows you how you can apply it not only to replicate the successful methods of others but also to create your own successes. NLP can also be used as a way of understanding the methods by which you achieve good results and how you can reproduce them on a consistent basis.

Thousands of people all over the world have already found NLP can create improved results in many areas of their life. In any of these areas, NLP can help you to make use of your inner potential, create a vision and purpose, set effective goals and achieve them.

How to use this book

This book is for anyone who wants to explore what NLP is about or who wants to know more about the techniques – anyone who wants to learn a process that can improve his quality of life.

Chapters 1 to 5 explain the basic principles of NLP. The following chapters go into detail about the different techniques that you can use to remove barriers and move towards success. Chapter 11 brings everything together and looks at how you might work with another person. There is also a useful glossary of NLP terms and a bibliography at the end of the book.

The aim of the book is that you will be able to use your new skills to improve your life. You can begin to use these skills straightaway. They are all tried, tested and highly practical. The more you are able to practise them, the better. You may find it useful to find opportunities to practise them as you go through the book, as you will find this helps your understanding grow. So do take the time to try them out with yourself or others.

Most importantly, NLP is about experimenting and enjoying new things, so have fun!

1 The basics of NLP

NLP is a way of thinking and a method for achieving excellence in your life. Its structure comes from modelling people who have already achieved success in many different areas. You can transfer these ways of thinking, doing and being to your life to achieve results. This chapter sets out the groundwork you need to know before you can start to apply NLP to your daily life. Whatever you have and are doing or being in your life is because of what you believe is true about the world. What would happen if you changed some of those beliefs?

What's in the name?

The name 'Neuro-Linguistic Programming' refers to the unconscious processes each person uses to produce behaviour – and therefore results. If you are not achieving the results you want, change your thinking and your behaviour will change.

Neuro

Each component of the name is important. The word 'neuro' refers to the nervous system. Our direct experience of the world comes to the brain via the nervous system and the five senses. The senses are the means by which we interact with the world:

▶ the visual sense – seeing
▶ the auditory sense – hearing
▶ the kinaesthetic sense – touch
▶ the olfactory sense – smell
▶ the gustatory sense – taste

One of the first things that NLP is concerned with is how we process this sensory experience and translate it into conscious and unconscious thought.

Linguistic

The second word in Neuro Linguistic Programming refers to language. Specifically it means the way in which we use language to order and give meaning to what we have experienced through the senses.

Communication – both verbal and non-verbal types – is the medium by which you express the unconscious and conscious thoughts you have about yourself, other people and the world around you as a whole.

must know

It's not what happens to you that's important. It's what you do with what happens that makes the difference.

Programming

The third word in Neuro Linguistic Programming looks at the consistent ways in which we think or behave. Just like a computer, each of us runs specific *programmes* to produce our behaviour. Programmes consist of a series of steps that automatically produce certain results in different circumstances.

You can use NLP to find out what particular programmes you run and what results they produce. It also gives you the means to change your own and other people's programmes to produce exactly the results you want.

The core of NLP

At the heart of NLP is a particular way of thinking. This holds that anyone can achieve success by learning how other people get their results. This is called *modelling*.

Modelling

To model someone, you identify a person who does something excellently and you observe how he does it, specifically by looking at, questioning and analysing him to discover:

▶ that person's language, i.e. the words he uses and the *structure* of his language
▶ his physiology, i.e. how he uses his body
▶ his thinking, beliefs and values, unconscious and conscious. (See *Putting it all together*, pages 179-85)

By copying what that person does in these three areas, you can also achieve excellent results. NLP has an efficient toolkit of techniques to help you do this.

must know

In essence, NLP consists of:
▶ a methodology – modelling
▶ a series of techniques

The history of NLP

Given the technical-sounding name, it is not surprising that Neuro-Linguistic Programming was invented by two academics. John Grinder, an assistant professor of linguistics at the University of Santa Cruz, California, and Richard Bandler, who had studied a range of subjects from Gestalt therapy to maths and computing, came together to see what they could learn about how people became effective.

Their influences

Bandler and Grinder drew on existing concepts and ways of thinking. Grinder was already experienced in modelling, as he had learned several languages through this method. The words 'Neuro Linguistic' came from Alfred Korsybski, 'thinker' and founder/author of General Semantics.

Another influential academic was the British anthropologist Gregory Bateson. He proposed that there was no such thing as reality. Instead he suggested each person unconsciously edited that person's perceptions of the world to fit his own beliefs. So he decided that if people could change their beliefs, they could produce different ways of acting in the world.

must know

Anything one person can do another person can do too. If one person can learn to do something well, so can another. It is simply a question of working out how someone else does it and learning the same strategies.

The models for NLP

Grinder and Bandler modelled three successful therapists who produced excellent results. What they were really interested in finding out was *the difference that made the difference*. In other words, what was it that set these people apart from the average? What was different about their thinking?

What was different about the way they behaved? How did this set up the successful results they achieved? The therapists whose work they looked at were Milton Erickson, Virginia Satir and Fritz Perls.

Milton Erickson

Milton Erickson (1901–80) had been a psychiatrist and was at the time a highly successful hypnotherapist. The way in which he used language and hypnosis has become known as 'Ericksonian hypnosis'.

NLP 'modelled' all Erickson's language to produce the Milton Model (see pages 104-15) of language patterns. These can be used to put another person into a light 'trance' – a useful state in which NLP techniques can produce change.

Virginia Satir

Virginia Satir (1916–88) was a family therapist who developed a new approach to working with families. She developed the idea of five key personality areas found in people's behaviour. These are known as 'Satir categories'. Many of her ideas have become common currency since her death.

Fritz Perls

Fritz Perls (1893–1970) is known as the founder of Gestalt Therapy, which he co-developed into a general therapeutic tool. He moved away from the psychoanalytical model in which the past is analysed and saw what was happening in the *present* as the key to change.

Taking it further

Out of the models that Bandler and Grinder produced came a series of techniques, and these form the strategies that can be used to change behaviour. They are outlined in the following chapters.

Where you are now and where you want to be

Change is a journey between where you are now and where you will be in the future. The way NLP expresses this is as the journey between the *present state* and the *desired state*.

Blocks to change

What stands between where you are now and where you want to be is an issue or problem to tackle. It may be a habit or particular behaviour you want to change. NLP discovers the programmes you are running and helps you *reprogramme* your unconscious mind to change that behaviour. The *instruction* to change comes from your *conscious* mind. But it is the *unconscious* mind that learns the new way of doing things and produces new behaviour.

The unconscious mind

So what is the unconscious mind? (NLP tends to refer to the unconscious rather than the subconscious mind, but both terms are generally used to mean the same thing.) The unconscious is everything that is not part of your conscious awareness. It is the home of your beliefs, motivations and behaviour. It acts in habitual, repeated ways.

You can give your conscious mind an instruction to change, but it is your unconscious mind that carries out the instruction. For example, imagine sitting down in a chair. You may tell yourself consciously to sit down, but it is your unconscious that relays the instructions to each individual muscle in your body at the same time and allows you to take that action.

must know

All change is unconscious. Change doesn't happen as a result of willpower. Changes in behaviour happen as a result of changes that are going on internally.

How we learn and change

There are four levels of change in learning:

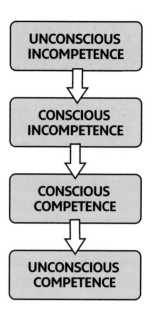

Unconscious incompetence

At this stage, you don't know how to do something but you don't even realize that you don't know how to do it. This is the blissful ignorance stage. For example, if you had never thought about driving, you would have no notion of what it would be like if you were to drive.

Conscious incompetence

At this stage, you become aware that you don't know something. When you try to drive for the first time you realise just how much there is to learn. The positive thing at this stage is that you can make rapid progress because you have so much to learn.

Conscious competence

By this stage, you have learned some skills. You are conscious that you have the skills needed for the task you are performing and are relatively competent. Progress is likely to be slower from now on, but that's only because there is less to learn now and what's left may be not as easy to acquire.

Your skills are not yet automatic, though. Take the driving example: as a new driver, if a passenger in the back seat talks too much, you may be put off a little. That's because you're still thinking about what you're doing. But you have still acquired the basics and can use them pretty well.

Unconscious competence - mastery

Now your skills have become unconscious. You can talk or listen to music while driving safely – your basic driving skills, looking in the mirror, changing gears and being aware of other cars on the road is done unconsciously, freeing up your conscious mind to focus on other things. This is the level at which you acquire mastery of a skill. The beliefs you have about what you are doing are also unconscious. By this stage, you simply believe that you are a driver – it has become part of your identity.

The four rules for success

Out of all the work done by the different developers of NLP a set of four rules has evolved that are sound principles for getting success. These four rules can be used to get what you want in any area of your life.

must know

The four rules for success:
1. Know what you want.
2. Take action to get it.
3. Be flexible.
4. Be aware.

Know what you want

NLP always starts with the final goal in mind because its core belief is that you will get whatever you focus on in life. If you don't know what you want, you are essentially acting like a boat without oars. Although you are going to get somewhere eventually, it won't be a place of your choosing. If you know where you want to go, you will know in which direction you should steer yourself. Always set out on your journey with a goal in mind.

Many people have goals but are not specific enough about what results they want. They may know what they want in a very general way or they may know what they do not want. In either case, their results are unlikely to be satisfactory. It is only if you think through what you want in a specific way that you will achieve very clear and precisely targeted results. (See Chapter 5, pages 80-91.)

Take action to get it

People who get the results they want do so by taking action towards their end goal, their desired outcome. They may not always have a complete plan, but they can start the journey because they have an end in mind.

Be flexible

If you are on track, keep doing more of the same. However if you don't seem to be getting the results you want, you can try something different. If you keep taking different actions, eventually you will get a different result that is close to the one you want to achieve.

Be tenacious. Keep going until you do achieve your final result. As long as you always keep the result you want in mind and are infinitely flexible in your behaviour, then eventually you will find the right methods to use to get it.

The process of modelling will help you to be flexible (see *The modelling process*, pages 182–83). If you have a model for a certain type of behaviour and success, then you will have a very clear example of the ways in which you need to change to get the result you want.

Be aware

To be flexible, you need sensory acuity. 'Sensory acuity' is basically a piece of jargon that means 'observe in detail what is going on using all your senses'. In other words, be aware in every situation. Ask yourself:

❏ What results are you getting from taking action towards your outcome?
❏ Does it seem to be working?
❏ Are you being effective?
❏ Is there something that you need to change?

These questions will help to stir you in the right direction to achieve your outcome – the result that you are aiming to achieve.

must know

NLP is *outcome oriented*. An *outcome* is the result you want to get in a specific context.

Empowering beliefs for creating change

Here are some ways of thinking about the world that you may find empowering.

A map is only a map

Every person has his own view, or map, of the world. This map is not the same as the territory it outlines – in other words, it is not objective truth. What you believe is true is just *your* perception of the world. If you start to believe that your map is objective reality rather than an individual perception, it will make you inflexible and therefore resistant to change.

Perceptions, on the other hand, are flexible and can be changed. By changing how you see the world (your map), you will be able to change the results you get in that world. NLP contains the toolkit by which you can change your map of the world.

Have respect for different models of the world

Because everybody has a unique model or map of the world, you are surrounded by people who see the same experience as you through different eyes. They have different ways of thinking. They may disagree with some of your beliefs or value different things in life.

The quality and depth of your relationships with other people is based on how much you respect these differences between another person's world and yours. Respect allows you to bridge the gap between your way of thinking and the other person's way of thinking and to communicate effectively with that person. Being effective in your communication makes you effective in your life.

A person's behaviour may be misinterpreted. We often confuse the behaviour someone exhibits with who he is as a person. As you will see throughout the book, a key principle behind NLP is that what someone *does* is not the same as who that person *is*.

People work perfectly

Everything you have in your life right now exists because you are *already* perfect at getting results. The programmes you are running are *all* effective. They *all* get results. These may not, of course, be the results you actually want. However, your unconscious mind is working perfectly, given the instructions it already has. It's the same for everyone. Everyone works perfectly.

People make the best choice(s) available

In general people will always make the best choices available to them. They do something because they think it will work. It may not get the result they want, of course, but they have made the best choice they can with their *current* abilities to use their *current* resources.

People already have the resources they need

We all have the ability to change our beliefs, goals and motivation. So we already have all the foundation resources we need to make the change we want. All that is required is that we have an attitude of flexibility and a willingness to experiment to learn new skills.

In NLP thinking, *there are no unresourceful people, only unresourceful states*. When you feel unresourceful, it doesn't mean that you have no resources, just that you aren't using them or you don't know how to access them. That is a way of *behaving*. It is very different from being an unresourceful *person*.

Because the majority of your resources are unconscious, it is important to learn to communicate with your unconscious mind so that you can harness them. NLP techniques give you ways to do this.

Underlying every behaviour is a positive intention

The unconscious works for our benefit, and everything it does has positive intention. So when you observe yourself or someone else behaving in a way that doesn't seem to be positive, you should look for the positive intent behind that person's actions.

For example, being rude to someone may not get the positive benefit of a happy reaction from that person, but it might make you feel assertive or honest. Eating a piece of pie may not help your diet, but it might make you feel happy to experience the taste in your mouth.

What you get is what you communicate

Have you ever talked to someone and found out later that they received a totally different message from the one you intended? Have you ever been unable to persuade a colleague to do something, even though your case seemed convincing? Has someone ever said something to you but seemed to imply something else? Have you ever ended up guessing what that might be? A dialogue between individuals is a process of feedback from one person to another about what each person *thinks* the other is saying.

You cannot *not communicate*. You may not realize it but you are always communicating. Even before you begin talking to someone, just the way you stand or sit is sending out a message to that person. The verbal and non-verbal response you get tells you what meaning he is giving to your communication.

In NLP, the person who wants a result takes responsibility for getting that result. You can learn techniques to understanding how different people interpret messages. This will enable you to change the way you communicate in order to ensure that they get the message you want to give them.

Rapport determines your success in communicating with another person

The amount of rapport you have with a person will determine your success in communicating a particular message to him. Rapport will essentially bring about the ability to influence another person.

When you are in deep rapport with someone, you will want to do what that person wants you to do because you perceive it to be in your interest. You will feel so aligned with the other person's way of thinking that you believe that what he wants must also be good for you. Equally, the deeper your rapport with another person, the greater your ability will be to influence him.

If someone resists your suggestions, then your rapport with that person is not deep enough. It is no good trying to coerce or manipulate the person. It won't work. To combat resistance, you will need to learn how to deepen your rapport with the person who is presenting resistance.

The person who is most flexible in his behaviour has the best chance of success

The more flexible you are in your behaviour, and the more you are willing to play and experiment, the more likely you will be able to establish rapport with people who think very differently from you. In fact, in any given situation, the person who is able to be most flexible in his thinking and behaviour is the one who will be most influential.

If you keep doing what you have always done, you will always get the same results. If you change what you do, the reaction of people around you will change and your own response will be different. Being flexible will stop you getting stuck in particular ways of thinking and behaving and you will become much more successful at getting the outcomes that you want.

Frameworks of thinking

The basic ways of thinking about the actions you take are sometimes referred to in NLP as *behavioural frames*.

Outcome versus blame

The first behavioural frame in NLP is to be oriented towards an outcome rather than a problem.

Blame frame

Some therapies will look to a person's past to find out *why* that person is not achieving what he wants to achieve. This practice focuses on the problem and is sometimes referred to as the *blame frame*. If you use the blame frame to tackle an issue, you are likely to end up asking *why* a lot. 'Why am I like this?' 'Why did I do this?' 'Why do I create these sorts of problems?' The implication of these types of questions is that someone is to blame.

Outcome frame

Being outcome oriented is sometimes referred to as the *outcome frame*. NLP is interested in outcomes. It is not interested in *why*. It is interested in *how*. It doesn't matter *what* you do. It does matter *how* you do it. If you know why you do something, you are just likely to find a justification to continue doing it. If you know how you do something, you can change it.

How versus why

The second behavioural frame is to ask questions that uncover how you do what you do:

- ❏ *How* do I do what I do now?
- ❏ *What* can I do differently in the future?
- ❏ *How* can I do it differently to achieve a different outcome?

Curiosity and experimentation

Curiosity

Adopting curiosity as an attitude will lead you to ask lots of questions. You might discover a way of doing things effectively as a result. If you are curious, you might want to find out: 'How do they do that?' 'What is it that makes that presenter, manager, athlete, doctor or academic so effective?' 'How could I do that too?'

Experimentation

Be willing to experiment. Experimentation means that you apply what you find out. It is only by experimenting with different ways of doing things that you can learn what results you get from doing one thing rather than another.

Assumptions

Many of us simply *assume* we know what we are going to get in any given context. Assumptions and expectations lead to pre-judging a situation. If you always know what you are likely to get, why try anything new? If you make assumptions about the world, it is unlikely that you will ever want to experiment. Why bother? Have outcomes instead of assumptions.

Choice

Curiosity and experimentation *increase choice*. They are the attitudes you had when you were a child and you had an open mind towards the world. When you want to know more and try new things, you are more likely to succeed, as more choices of behaviour will be open to you.

Feedback versus failure

NLP is focused on *results*. If what you are doing is not working for you it doesn't mean you have failed. You have achieved results – just different ones from those you set out to achieve.

In NLP, everything that happens to us is information we can learn from. So take whatever happens to you as *feedback* on how near you are to the outcome you want. Life is full of setbacks. The key is whether you see them as opportunities to get new results or as failures.

Failure

Believing you can fail will probably lead you to experience negative emotions about yourself if you don't get what you want. These will then stop you from taking further action.

> Belief in failure
> = lack of choice / being stuck

> Belief in feedback = learning,
> new choices, action then results

People who get hung up on the idea of failure are likely to beat themselves up for not getting the result straightaway, which means they don't learn what they need to learn to change their actions. Then the whole process of moving forward becomes a struggle. All in all, it is not a very useful belief to hold.

Feedback

Belief in experience as *feedback* leads to an attitude of flexibility and the likelihood of more positive emotions. If you appear to be a long way away from your goal, simply be flexible and do something else – anything else. Feedback means that you have an opportunity to learn from your experience and to create a clearer path towards what you *do* want.

Possibility versus necessity

In NLP, it is useful to assume that there are always choices available. Assuming that something 'has to' or 'should' be done limits choice and flexibility. Looking for choices and possibilities makes you the *cause* rather than the *effect* of any situation.

Cause and effect

For every event that takes place we can assume that there is a cause, i.e. something created the effect. If we believe that we are affected by causes outside our control, we will not take responsibility for the results we create. We become victims of fate. NLP calls this *at effect*.

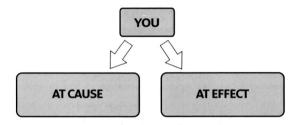

You'll recognize people who are *at effect* by their language:
'I am fat because I have a slow metabolism. There's nothing I can do about it.'
'There are no jobs around for people my age.'
'Men/women are all confused now, that's why I can't stay in a relationship. They don't want a proper relationship.'

These sentences all place the person as the victim of happenstance. It doesn't make them happy or resourceful.

If you decide to be *at cause* of whatever happens, on the other hand, you switch your thinking around and assume that you can influence what happens next. For example:
'My metabolism is slow but I can change it through exercise.'
'Many employers don't want people my age but I will find the exception to the rule.'
'What sort of person does want a relationship? How can I attract that person?'

To change your thinking, ask yourself: *'What can I do differently to get the result I want?'* This allows you to stay at the cause side of the equation and operate within NLP's four rules for success (see page 16).

2 Your internal world

We each have an individual map of what we call life. This is what gives us the results we get. How do you look at the world? In what way is that different from how others look at the world and why? In this chapter, you can learn more about what goes on in your internal world. The NLP term *state* means the way you feel at any particular moment. The emotional state you are in changes all the time. Learning to control your state is essential if you want to change your life.

Communication

You are a unique individual. You experience the world in a different way from everyone else. This is because you have your own set of rules that govern how you interact with people, how you talk to yourself and the choices you make for yourself about what to focus on. These rules are essentially about communication.

Information overload
The external world is a world of information. Every moment you are alive you are being bombarded with information through your five senses.

Every second around two million bits of information have to be processed. Obviously, it would be too much for you to cope with if you were consciously aware of all this information. So you have to filter some of the information out. You do this entirely unconsciously.

A model of communication
In NLP the description of what goes on in your internal world when you interact with the external world is known as the *communication model*.

Filters
Each person has their own unique set of filters to handle everything that is coming in from the outside world. Your filters are your way of making sense of what you are experiencing. They include what you believe, what you want, what you remember and what is important to you. These change over time and so your map of the world changes too.

Internal representation

The information that passes from the external world through your filters is held as an *internal representation*. Internal representations are our thoughts made up of pictures, feelings, sounds, smells and tastes. They are our experience of the world.

Your internal world determines:
▶ your state – that is, your particular mindset and emotions
▶ your body language (in NLP terms *physiology*) – posture, breathing and facial expressions
▶ your behaviour – the actions you take in the outside world.

All are inter-related. The state you are in affects your behaviour. The internal representations you have affect your state and physiology. Your state, behaviour and physiology determine how you experience life at any moment. By changing any of these, you can change how you live life.

must know

Your internal representations make up your map of the world.

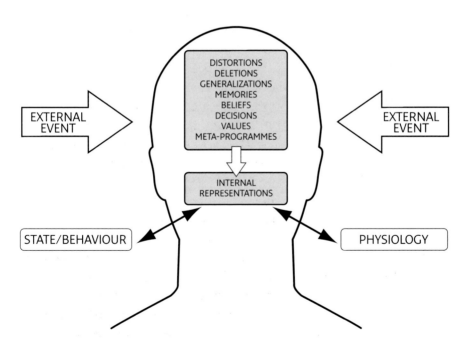

Deletion, generalization and distortion

How do we experience the outside world? First of all, each external event is experienced as information through the means of the five senses: seeing, hearing, feeling, taste and smell. As we have seen, you have to screen the vast majority of that data out for your own efficiency and survival. Let's look at how that happens.

Deletion

The first way in which the nervous system deals with a potential overload of information is to delete some of it. If you didn't do so, you would overload your conscious mind with sensory information.

Although a lot of information enters your brain, you only pay conscious attention to some parts of that information and overlook or cut out all the other bits. Everything that is deleted falls out of your conscious awareness.

Examples of deletion

You have probably had the experience of discovering a new food that you never knew existed before. Suddenly you begin to notice it whenever you go to the shops, even though you had never seemed to notice it before. What if someone tells you about an item of clothing that is currently fashionable? Until they mentioned it, you wouldn't have paid attention to it. You would just have filtered it out. The things you have deleted from your mind have always been there – you simply hadn't noticed them until you were reminded consciously to pay attention to them.

Why deletion is important

Imagine the implications of this process of deletion. Because what you focus on in life is what you get, when you decide you want something different, you can change what you are focusing on and what you delete. This will give you different results. Suppose you were a woman who wanted to be in a relationship but had previously ignored men over six feet as being too tall for you. You would stop deleting men of six feet tall and begin instead to focus on them. So in this way you would widen your options.

Implications of deletion

Issues arise when you don't realize you are deleting things and you delete something that would give you more choice in a particular situation – such as in the above example of the six-foot man.

Generalization

When you generalize, you reduce the amount of information you need to deal with by labelling it and slotting it into a category or a class. Generalization can be a very useful ability. Scientists, mathematicians and artists all use this technique.

When you are a child one of the ways you learn and develop your skills is through generalization. You probably generalized the world around you so that you did not have to cope with too much difference.

Examples of generalization

Imagine, for example, you are walking along the road and you see an animal that looks like a cat. You've seen a cat before, so you have a word for it already. Your brain says, 'I know that animal. It has got a tail and ears and makes a purring sound. It is quite big, but I already have a category called "cats" that is broad enough to allow both small and big cats in it.'

Your brain can also run other categories as an alternative: 'Could it be a wild cat like a lion or a tiger? No, it doesn't seem to be as big as any of the cats in that category and it seems to be too friendly. So I am putting it in my domestic cat category.'

There the cat stays, generalized away into your domestic cat category until the moment it does something quite uncat-like such as bark like a dog, at which point you might have to reassess the broad conclusion you drew about it earlier!

Implications of generalization

It is easy to see how useful it is to be able to categorize things. Imagine if you had to come up with a new word for every object or experience you had. However, generalizing can be limiting or dangerous too. It can make you rigid in your thinking and unprepared to notice exceptions to the rules. If you tend to generalize a lot, you can eliminate choice and opportunity by assuming that a past experience will be repeated in the future, for example: 'I lost money when I had that relationship therefore future relationships will make me poor.' Or 'People who look at me with that expression don't like me.'

Notice when an experience no longer fits into a category. When a cat barks, is it still a cat? When several people look at you in that way, does that still mean that they don't like you? Once you begin to realize how much you generalize experiences, you can see the patterns in what you do and also notice new information you might have been ignoring. That will allow you to look at how useful your existing categories are.

Distortion

Distortion occurs when you take the information that has come through the senses and draw a conclusion from it. For example, you may give it a particular interpretation, label or meaning. You may distort what you see, what you hear or what you feel. On a day-to-day level, when someone says something to you, you may distort it in your mind and remember having heard something different from what it was that they actually said.

Examples of distortion

An example of distortion is the well-known story in Eastern philosophy. A man walking along the road sees what he believes to be a snake and yells in fear, *'Snake!'* However, upon arriving at that place he realizes that it is really only a piece of rope. He has distorted what he has seen.

Another example of distortion may happen when you are alone in a strange house. Every house has sounds in it – creaking, pipes squeaking, sounds outside the house. Normally, in your own house or in a familiar environment, you delete those sounds because you are so used to them. But in a strange house sometimes you may focus on the sounds and even begin to distort them in your mind. Is that a pipe or a water tap? Is that a burglar you can hear? Is that a creak of a floorboard or someone talking? Your brain may be distorting those sounds and making them much louder than they would normally be.

Implications of distortion

Distortion is a positive and necessary part of any creative or artistic process. For example if you want to enjoy looking at art or entering the world of a book or losing yourself in music, you need to be able to distort your sensory input by putting more focus on one aspect of it than another.

There is a downside of distortion, however, if you jump too readily to a conclusion that has a negative implication for you. For example, a man sees his best friend talking to his girlfriend. He immediately distorts their expressions so that he thinks they 'look guilty' and therefore 'must have something to hide' and therefore 'must be having an affair'. In fact, the friend was asking the girlfriend for tips on where to buy the man a present.

Or, imagine you are giving a presentation to a large number of people. The audience watch you silently as you speak. What do you see in their blank faces? You might read their expressions as acceptance or rejection of what you are saying depending on what you believe. When you tell someone about the experience later you distort what happened.

Piecing it together

The issue with the filter processes of deletion, generalization and distortion is that they all happen within a matter of seconds, and they are unconscious. We don't even know when we are doing them.

One piece of information...

To get an idea of what's happening, let's take a look at how one piece of information passes through all three filters of deletion, generalization and distortion. Here's a story:

You see your boss talking to the managing director of your company in the office. He is smiling. Then he notices you and says, 'I have a new job to offer you. It will mean a promotion and a rise in salary.' He hurries off with a cheery expression on his face.

This seems like great news on the surface. However, you know that the last person who had a promotion was given the task of making a whole sub-office redundant and was then made redundant himself. You distort your boss's smile and assume that he was gloating. You delete the memory of all the positive things that both your boss and the managing director have said to you over the last few months. You delete the fact that the person who was made redundant had a very different career history from your own.

'Why did he hurry off?' you begin to think. 'There must be something he's hiding.' Now you start generalizing. You have to choose between two broad categories: 'great career opportunities' and 'things that have gone wrong in my career'.

At other times you would probably reassess what you had just seen and categorize the experience under 'great career experiences.' However, recently the economy has turned down, so you have noticed a lot of information about job losses. That hadn't bothered you until two of your friends lost their jobs last month. A month ago you had started looking out for signs things might be getting worse at your employer's. Your division had been doing well, but if you were sent to another division, how could you survive? You begin to use other information to distort your own situation.

You file the experience to fit with your current view of the world: 'You can't trust employers – they're out for what they can get.' You have just been offered promotion and a rise in salary and you have ended up feeling bitter and cynical!

Listen to your language

How can you begin to notice deletions, generalizations and distortions? Start by listening to your language. The words you use can give you vital clues to how you are thinking.

For example, if you hear yourself using phrases like 'I've seen this before', you may well be generalizing. Ask yourself, 'How is it different this time?' or 'What can I do differently this time?' or 'Would this really be the same in a different situation or context?'

The Meta model (see pages 98-103) provides a series of questions that can be used to find out how other people are deleting, distorting or generalizing information.

Forget the negatives – remember the positives

You are told not to think of a green bus. What happens? You think of a green bus. When the brain makes an internal representation (IR), it has to make a positive picture first before it can negate it. You cannot *not* think of something that you don't want to think about – you always think about it first!

So pay attention to the pictures you are really making inside your mind. Every time you say 'I don't want a green bus in my life any more', you are making an IR of a green bus and your behaviour, state and physiology will be determined by the thoughts of the green bus you don't want. To change your life, how about thinking of the red buses you want in your life instead?

Representational systems

One of the ways we process information is by choosing to pay more attention to information that comes through one sense rather than another. The experience we have of the outside world through our senses is represented *internally* as images. For example, you can make an internal visual image, an internal sound or a feeling. The means by which we do this are called *representational systems*.

must know

Constructing a visual image is known as Visual Construct (Vc). Remembering a visual image is known as Visual Remembered (Vr). Constructing an auditory image is known as Auditory Construct (Ac). Remembering an auditory image is known as Auditory Remembered (Ar). Talking to yourself is known as Auditory Digital (Ad).

Memories and constructed images

Information that is received through the senses in the form of internal images, sounds or feelings can be divided up further into memories and constructed images. Remember what your bedroom looks like – a visual memory – or imagine what it would look like if you changed the colour – a visual image. Both images will be represented internally.

The representational systems

Sight – the visual system

If you want to use your visual system, think of somewhere you have been in the past, remember a dream or imagine what your life will look like in the future. In each case, a picture comes to mind.

Hearing – the auditory system

When you talk to yourself, remember a piece of music or imagine what your voice will sound like as you get older you are using the auditory system.

Feeling – the kinaesthetic system

The kinaesthetic system includes your emotions, the feelings inside your body and your sense of touch. Imagine what it feels like to stroke a cat, to feel happy inside or to walk along a beach – you are using the kinaesthetic representational system.

Taste - the olfactory system

When you imagine what freshly baked bread smells like, or the smell of coffee or a favourite perfume, you are using your olfactory system.

Smell - the gustatory system

When you remember the taste of your breakfast this morning or imagine what a food you have never eaten might taste like you are using your gustatory system to make images.

Your preferred representational system

People may switch from one representational system to another from moment to moment, but they may still have a preference for using one way of communicating information. You make distinctions about the world most within your preferred system. For example, if your preferred system is visual then you will remember and construct more visual than sound or feeling images.

Your preferred representational system also determines what language you use most frequently. So, if you can listen to language, you can identify it. Likewise, if you can identify the preferred representational system of the people you meet, you can learn how to 'speak their language' and deepen your relationships.

Your lead representational system

Your lead representational system is different from your preferred representational system. While the preferred system is the one you use the majority of the time, the lead system is the one that you use *first of all* when you want to access information. Your lead system will be visual, auditory or kinaesthetic. For example, if you were asked to remember your journey to work today, you might first of all go inside to access your feelings about it, remember what it looked like or remember the sounds you experienced during the journey.

Eye patterns or accessing cues

To determine what representation system someone is using at a particular time, as well as listening to that person's language you can look at the direction in which his eyes are moving. These are known as *eye patterns* or *eye accessing cues*.

Thought processes and eye movements

When someone moves his eyes in a certain direction, that person is accessing a certain mode of thinking. This is easiest to see on someone else, so the pictures given here are as if you are looking at someone else. If you try to follow your own accessing cues, you will probably tie yourself up in knots!

Visual cues

If you look at another person who is imagining or constructing a visual image, you will notice how that person unconsciously moves his eyes up and to his right. If you notice him moving his eyes up and to his left, he is remembering a visual image. If that person looks straight ahead at you with unfocused eyes, he is in 'visual defocused', thinking in a series of pictures.

Auditory cues

If someone moves his eyes sideways to his right, that person is thinking about how something will sound in the future. If you notice him moving his eyes to his left, he is remembering a sound or something someone said in the past. If the person moves his eyes down and to the left, he is talking to himself (auditory digital).

Kinaesthetic cues

If you notice a person looking down and to his right, that person will be accessing a feeling or asking himself, 'How do I feel about what I have seen or heard?'

QUESTIONS FOR EYE PATTERNS

VISUAL CONSTRUCTED IMAGES
'What would your bathroom look like if you painted it blue?'

VISUAL REMEMBERED IMAGES
'What did your bathroom look like six months ago?'

CONSTRUCTED SOUNDS
'What would your voice sound like if you had a mask over it?'

REMEMBERED SOUNDS
'What does your best friend sound like when he is talking?'

KINAESTHETIC
(FEELINGS AND BODILY SENSATIONS)
'What does it feel like when you touch a soft blanket?'

AUDITORY DIGITAL
(INTERNAL DIALOGUE)
'Recite a joke or poem to yourself'

THIS IS AS YOU LOOK AT SOMEONE ELSE

To test a person's eye accessing cues, ask them questions that will cause them to construct or remember feelings, sounds and images or internal dialogue

Language and the senses

Different representational systems use different key words, known in NLP as *predicates*. Predicates are sensory-specific words. They include verbs, adverbs and adjectives.

Predicates

People will habitually use the language that goes with their preferred representational systems and use least the language that goes with their least preferred representational system.

Sensory clues

As well as words, people who primarily use the visual sense share other features. They tend to talk quickly, breathe high in the chest and are often thin and stand up straight. Because they think by making pictures in their head they will understand you better if you show them pictures.

People who habitually use the kinaesthetic sense can be spotted by their slow speaking, deep breathing from low in the stomach and the fact that they tend to stand closer to others and like to touch people.

An auditory preference may be spotted in someone who breathes from the middle of the chest. They learn by listening and find it easy to repeat what someone has said to them. Often their voices have a lot of melody in them and they enjoy speaking on the telephone, where they are not distracted by the other senses, though they are put off by noise.

In auditory digital (non-sensory specific) mode, the person shows a mixture of the features of all the other systems.

Predicates

Visual words and phrases

Look, see, show, clear, bright, picture, clarify, vision, highlight, perspective, illustrate, focus, colourful, seems, survey, dark, scene, spotlight, shadow, vivid, foresee, appearance, watch, illusion, shine, dim, reflect, obscure, eye, sparkle, vivid, watch, dark, light. I see what you are saying. That's true beyond the shadow of a doubt. You can really get a bird's eye view here. That's how it appears to me. In my mind's eye. I have a dim view of it. You're making a scene. I'm getting a perspective on it. In light of your argument... In view of what you say...

Auditory words and phrases

Noise, hear, resonate, deaf, talk, dissonance, harmonize, speak, rhythm, ask, silent, tune, pitch, clear, buzz, click, audible, earful, proclaim, vocal, cry, say, tell, sound, quiet, discuss, whine, growl, melodious, monotonous, remark, sigh, hum, dumb, call. I am all ears. That rings a bell. It strikes a chord with me. That was quite an earful. Hold your tongue. That's right in a manner of speaking. Lend me your ear a moment. It's as clear as a bell.

Auditory digital words

Sense, think, decide, criteria, process, motivate, learn, mention, perceive, consider, change, conceive.

Kinaesthetic words and phrases

Feel, touch, grab, unfeeling, solid, concrete, hit, handle, tackle, pressure, topsy-turvy, hothead, handle, sticky, scrape, grasp, soft, hard, cold, hot, tackle, solid, concrete, contact, push, pull, gentle, sensitive, tickle, warm, smooth, sharp, seize, pressure. I got hold of this idea. Can you get a handle on it? I made contact with them. I am going to lay my cards on the table. It slipped my mind. I will have to start from scratch. It's a real pain in the neck. Have you caught on to it yet? Can we turn this around?

did you know?

As well as the auditory preference there seems to be a group of people who have a distinct preference for self-talk (auditory digital) as their main representational system. This way of thinking also has its own set of key words.

Your state and the world

The word 'state' generally refers to 'emotional state': the moods and feelings you experience at any one time. A state comes about because of all the different thoughts, feelings and emotions you have in one moment.

The effects of your state

What is your state right now? Are you happy, sad, angry, exhilarated, upset, depressed, joyous, energized, curious, excited or interested? The state you are in has an immediate effect on your behaviour, the way other people perceive you and the experiences you have as a result. Your state affects the way you see the world.

Every time your state of mind changes, the world outside will appear to change too. You will experience the world differently when you are feeling angry than when you are feeling super-confident. You will also behave differently. How you feel internally affects everything about the way you experience the external world and the results you get.

While you may not be aware that you have any control over how you feel, in fact you can learn to be more consciously in charge of the state you are in at all times. This is because your state is determined by the pictures you make inside you (your internal representations) and by how you hold your body. You can learn to change your pictures and posture, and so change your state. NLP has several techniques to help you do this. (See *Changing state*, pages 44–45.)

State and physiology

The state of mind you are in affects how you hold your body: your posture, how you walk, how you sit, the angle at which you hold your head or your spine. Think about how you shift your position when you feel sad. How about when you feel happy or angry?

You will probably notice how much your body shifts when you change state. Imagine you had had a terrible day, then you suddenly had a call telling you about something exciting that was about to happen, or a friend walked in with an enormous present for you. Or how about if you just put some music on and started dancing? Your state would change instantly, and without you having to think about it.

Your baseline/habitual state

Of course sometimes you feel good and sometimes not so good. At the extremes your state can move from depression to happiness or from anger to joy. In between these extremes, is a state that you are probably in most of the time.

The state you are in most of the time is known as your *baseline state*. This is how you 'are' and how you 'feel' most of the time. *What* your baseline state is is determined by how you see the world the majority of the time.

Working with others

When you work with other people using NLP techniques, it is important to be conscious of changes in state – both in yourself and the other person. You will also learn how to induce a state in yourself and others. Bringing about a state at will allows you to get effective results using techniques such as anchoring (see pages 130–37).

must know

There are no unresourceful people, only unresourceful states.

Changing state

Many states appear to be determined by external events, but you can choose the state you are in as well. How do you do it?

Changing what you are thinking about can change your state

First, if you change the pictures you make inside, you can change your state. When you change your internal pictures, this in turn affects you outwardly – it changes your physiology and how you behave. The way you behave in turn changes the results you get.

Changing your internal pictures to change state

Here is a technique for changing the pictures inside your head and therefore changing your emotional state:

▶ Think of a time in the past when something happened to you that you weren't happy about.

▶ Notice how you feel when you think about this experience.

▶ Now notice how you are holding your body.

▶ CLEAR THE INTERNAL PICTURE SCREEN.

▶ Now, remember a particular time in the past when you felt happy or super-confident.

▶ Notice how you feel as you remember what happened.

▶ Now notice how you are holding your body.

  Learn how making negative and positive pictures in your mind affects your body and your state.

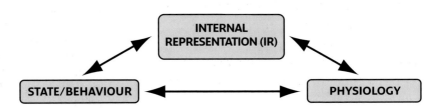

Changing your physiology can change your state

This process works in reverse too. If you change your body language first, it will change how you feel inside. This in turn will change the pictures you are making inside, which will change your state.

Changing your physiology to change your state

▶ Consider how you would like to feel at the moment.

▶ For example, if you want to achieve a goal, how about feeling totally motivated?

▶ Or, if you are about to talk to your partner, how about feeling totally loving?

▶ Now SHAKE YOUR BODY OUT to lose whatever state you are currently in.

▶ Shift your body until you get the feeling of being totally motivated or totally loving. You can sit, stand upright or move to get into 'state'.

▶ Take a deep breath and breathe the way you would if you were in the state.

▶ Change your facial expression to match your desired state.

You can change how you feel

Actors know this, of course. If you watch a film, notice how they shift their bodies to show a change of mood. This will work in real life too. You can immediately change your state by shifting your body until you get the right physiology for the state of mind you want to be in.

Think about it. You can't be excited if your body is curled up in a sad, depressed shape. Likewise, you can't be sad if you are jumping around with your hands in the air, your head held up high and your spine straight. You might feel happy, confident or excited, though!

Choosing states

Choosing what state you are in can open up a world of new possibilities and bring you new results.

How to choose a positive state

What is it like when you feel a little down or demotivated? Think about your posture. You are probably slumping or hanging your head and looking down. You might be telling yourself how terrible you are or the world is.

But if you want to feel happy, you can change this negative feeling instantly. Stop whatever you are doing. Straighten your spine. Look up. Put a big smile on your face. Shout out loud, 'Fantastic! Wonderful!' You will feel it too!

Using your state to get results

Whatever the situation, changing your state from a negative to positive one will give you results. You aren't going to be able to do a fantastic business presentation if you feel unconfident. You won't make a new friend if you walk into a room looking and feeling angry at the world. However you *will* sell something if you feel powerful and positive about selling. And you *will* make a new friend if you are relaxed and happy and loving. If you want something new in your life, changing state will help you to get it.

Interview states

Imagine you are going for an interview or an important meeting. Are you are a little nervous about the questions that will be asked? How would you like to feel instead? What would be a useful state to be in? Relaxed? Confident? Cheerful? Happy?

You can 'mentally rehearse' your interviews in advance. Wherever you are just visualize walking into the room. Talk to yourself:

▶ State how you would like to feel in positively expressed language, for example 'I would like to feel confident' (rather than 'I would not like to be nervous').

▶ Now think of a specific time when you felt like this in the past.

▶ Haven't got one? Imagine what it would be like if you were feeling confident or cheerful or happy or whatever state you would find most useful right now.

▶ Try it on for size to get the memory back (or the imagined feeling in place). Feel it, hear what you did hear (or would hear), see what you did hear (or would hear) *as if you were there right now*.

▶ You will probably find that you have to adjust your body to get into the right state. Maybe you will change the way you are sitting, the angle of your head, arms or legs, or your facial expression. Practise in your head and then actually do it on the day.

Now you are in a resourceful state, you will be sure to have a successful interview.

Learning state

Have you ever learned something incredibly easily and effortlessly? There are times when we just pick up knowledge without really thinking about it – it just seems to be absorbed without any effort of will and we are able to recall it whenever we want to. However at other times it is much more difficult to learn. That is because learning is linked to the state we are in at the time.

Two people might give you the same information, but you will respond differently to them because of their different states. The state you are in at the time you hear the information will affect how efficiently you learn that information. If you have ever learned from someone who had no interest in the subject they were teaching you, you'll remember the difference between that experience and learning from someone who was excited or deeply passionate about the subject they were teaching.

Association and dissociation

There are two ways of experiencing states. In NLP, they are known as *association* and *dissociation*.

Association

When you really experience a state, you are *associated into* it. You feel as if the state is happening to you *right now*. When you are fully associated into what you are doing, you often lose your sense of time because you are so absorbed by the experience.

Remember something pleasant that has happened to you in the past. Imagine that you are actually experiencing now what you experienced at that time. See it through your own eyes, feel what you felt and hear what you heard. When you are in the experience, be it a present event, a remembered past event or an imagined future event, you can associate into it to really feel what it is like, was like or will be like.

Dissociation

Dissociation is when you are the observer of an experience – in other words, you remain at a distance from the emotions generated by it, so that you don't fully experience that state. You are thinking about it rather than actually being in it. With dissociation, when you remember or imagine a past or future experience, you will see a picture of the experience with *you* in it – as if it is a film – rather than a physical experience that is happening to you. You may still have feelings about what you are observing, but they will be different from those you would feel if you were actually associated into the experience.

There are times when it is useful to be dissociated. For example, if you want to review an unpleasant past memory so that you can learn what you need to learn from it without experiencing the emotions of the past, you would choose to dissociate from it. It may be useful to step outside an experience you are over-associated into in the present as well.

Changing others' states

As well as changing your own state, you can change other people's states as well. If you are using NLP with someone else and that person gets himself into an intense negative state, it is important to be able to help him out of that state and into a positive state.

Being aware of other people's states

How does a confident person stand? How does a nervous person sit? Body language shows how a person may be feeling at a particular moment.

Pattern interrupts

When a person has got into a negative pattern of behaviour, you can interrupt that pattern by doing something totally unexpected. This will immediately distract the person and he will dissociate from the state he was in. For example, what would happen if a child was having a tantrum and you threw yourself on the floor and had one too?

Break state

Breaking state is changing from an intense state to a neutral state. This gives you the space to choose another state to change to. You can break state by just doing something that distracts you from the *state* you are in, for example looking at something else in the room or standing up and moving around so that your physiology changes.

> **watch out!**
>
> Laughter is a great way to break someone's state. However, make sure that you are in rapport with him if you do this (see the following chapter), otherwise you will annoy the person, as you will appear unsympathetic.

Breaking others' states

If you are with someone else and need to change his state quickly, you can:

▶ ask that person to stand up, move around or have a glass of water
▶ point to something out of the window or in the room
▶ make a noise, or say something that takes his attention away from what he is doing
▶ make him laugh

3 Unconscious filters

What makes you look at the world in the way you do? You filter your experience of life through your beliefs, values and attitudes as well as your memories and a set of deep motivational filters called *Meta programmes*. Change these to create new results.

Beliefs and behaviour

One way to bring about change is to learn a new skill. If you want to learn to build a house you may need to learn bricklaying or architecture or carpentry. How about if you are shy and want to learn to be confident? Here you need to effect deeper changes in your attitude to life. This means looking at the unconscious filters that motivate you including your beliefs.

must know

Beliefs determine what you pay attention to. What you pay attention to guides your behaviour.

Beliefs

Beliefs are deeply held opinions or views about the world – what we hold to be a 'truth' or 'fact'. They are generalizations we have made about the world, and the important thing to recognize about them is that, as such, they are simply a map of how the world is, not the territory.

New beliefs are formed as we go through life. They may be changed, discarded or become stronger and more resistant to change.

How beliefs are formed

The beliefs we hold are formed unconsciously at different times and from different sources. When you are a child you are exposed to your family's ways of thinking about the world. Even if they never talked directly about what they believed, you would still have picked up their way of thinking by the way they acted and would have formed opinions based on those unconscious messages.

New beliefs are formed from any strong experience that has the ability to make you think about life in a different way. When you first go to school or university or work you may encounter new areas of life about which you have no existing opinions. If you don't have a framework to fit them into, you will form a new belief about the subject.

How beliefs impact your behaviour

An interesting thing about beliefs is their relationship to what we see, hear, taste, smell and feel. You might presume that your beliefs and opinions would change as a direct result of the information that came to you through your senses. In fact, we delete and distort that information *according* to our beliefs.

Every time something happens, you only notice the information that proves your existing belief, making it self-fulfilling and resilient to change unless a big life experience comes in that you can't fit into your existing model of the world. In other words, beliefs help to create the reality around us. Then you act according to the reality you have created.

How you reinforce your existing beliefs

An example of how this works is with obesity. One person will say, 'I am overweight because I have a slow metabolism and I am genetically predisposed to be overweight.' These factors may well be present. But because the person believes them to be an absolute truth, he won't make diet and lifestyle changes because he 'knows' whatever he does will be doomed to fail.

However, a second person may have the same factors present but believe that he can change his fate because he has seen someone else do it. So he will investigate what foods are unsuitable for him and what kind of exercise will be best help him. Because he *believes* he can change, he takes *actions* that will help him to change.

Core beliefs

Some beliefs are so deeply held that they are considered *core beliefs*. These are so much part of the way we see the world and so unconscious that we never question them.

Identifying your beliefs

A core belief could be an opinion such as 'People are all different.' If someone holds this belief, he will look for evidence in the world around him to reinforce this view. A secondary belief arising from this could be something like 'People are different, therefore I am different, therefore I can't be as successful as others.' So an opinion that may initially appear to be neutral may in fact limit us enormously.

Core beliefs are essential to our identity. Each core belief may be surrounded by clusters of (secondary) beliefs that support them. How can we identify them?

▶ Stop for a moment and focus on your beliefs.

▶ What opinions do you hold? What do you believe is true about your work? Your relationships? Your friends? Your social life?

▶ Is it useful for you to believe that?

▶ How do you think your beliefs are different from or similar to those of the people in your life?

▶ If you were to change a belief, how might that change the actions you take?

'Good' and 'bad' beliefs

There is no such thing as a 'good' or 'bad' or 'right' or 'wrong' belief, only a 'useful' and 'not useful' belief. You may have a set of beliefs that work very well for you. However, if your situation or life circumstances change, they may no longer prove to be useful.

Take the notion 'I am a nice person who always thinks about others.' This would seem to be a very positive belief that would produce positive behaviour. Yet what does 'thinking about others' really mean? Maybe it means putting other people's needs first. It might be appropriate to think about other people's needs, but not if your needs are forgotten. What if you change jobs and 'thinking about others' means that you can't make a decision without other people's approval? Your new job requires you to make tough decisions about hiring and firing people. How will that fit into your belief about being 'nice'?

Decisions

Every time you make a decision you change or reinforce a belief. Your beliefs will grow from every decision that you take. For example, suppose when you are very young you decide wealth is good. You will start early on in your life to take actions to become rich. Imagine a woman who decides early in life that 'all men are bastards'. Later in life she will have very unhappy relationships as she attempts unconsciously to prove that original decision was correct.

Changing your beliefs

To change a belief may be very simple. As an example, you tell me, 'This is the street the bank is on.' I walk down it with you and there is no bank. You may struggle for a few moments with your memory but will have to admit that you were wrong. Sometimes you can't change one belief without changing a string of others. Once upon a time most people in Europe believed that the world was flat. Even when they were told it was round they weren't convinced because it didn't fit into their series of beliefs about life. These other beliefs had to change first. Now most of us believe the world is round because we are taught it at school and we have seen pictures of it. It would take a lot to persuade us that this wasn't true.

In *Removing blocks* (see pages 139–57), we will look at how to use specific techniques to change your deeply held core beliefs and produce change in your life.

Values – the reason why

Values are another unconscious filter through which we look at the world. Values are *what are important to us*. They are what motivates us and gives us a reason *why* we do what we do. They are the standards by which we live.

Different values for different areas of life

Love, health, happiness, learning, challenge and relationships can all be values. We may have different values for different areas of our lives. For example:

▶ Your *life values* are the reason why you choose to live your life in the way you do.

▶ Your *relationship values* are the reasons why you choose to have one sort of relationship rather than another.

▶ Your *work values* determine why you choose one job rather than another.

▶ Your *health values* motivate you in your choices of both food and exercise.

Where values come from

Values develop out of our personal experiences, just like beliefs. Some come from the values that your family instilled in you when you were young. If your family believed it was important to be nice to your neighbours, you may value living in a closely knit neighbourhood later in life. It may prove to be an important factor in the choice you make about the location of your home.

Some of your values may become very different from those of your family as you get older. That's because you will also be influenced by other people and experiences: your friends, the media, your education and any different cultures you come into contact with.

Three key stages

It is believed that there are three key ages at which we change our values:

1. *The imprint period* lasts from the moment you are born up until you are seven. At this young age, you soak up values unconsciously from the people you are with most of the time. You are 'imprinted' with your family's values.

2. The second stage – *the modelling period* – is from around the age of 7 to 14. Your world generally gets bigger as you go to school and you are influenced by the wider variety of people you meet and look up to. These people may have different values from you.

3. The third stage – *the socialization period* – is from around the age of 14 to 21. At this age, we can exercise much more critical judgement about what we value. We have to choose how we are going to find a place in society and therefore which of our original values we may want to reject or replace. At this stage, you may find yourself in conflict with your friends, family or work colleagues.

VALUES

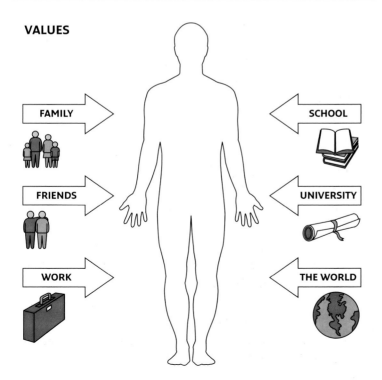

Carrot and stick

We are motivated by two types of values: values that pull us *towards* something, and values that push us *away from* something – carrots to tempt us or sticks to spur us on.

'Towards' and 'away from' values

For example, if you want more 'joy' or 'love' in your life, these are positively expressed and therefore *towards* values. However if you work only because you *'don't want* to be poor' rather than because you 'want to be rich', then you are motivated by an *away from* value.

The unconscious processes by forming pictures, so if it hears the statement 'I don't want X', it first of all forms an internal representation of what it *doesn't* want. So, if your value is 'not wanting to get poor' then your internal representation is of 'poor'. Therefore your unconscious keeps filtering for the thing you *don't* want, the picture of 'poor'. You may keep finding that money slips through your fingers or that you never make it at all.

What's important to you?

Suppose you get to a certain point in your life, yet you still aren't happy. Perhaps you have millions in the bank. Perhaps you have a great family, a big house, all the trappings of success. If this all still leaves you feeling empty, then it's because you don't have a life that really matters to *you*.

---

must know

To make the changes you want in life, you need to get a picture of what you *want* instead of what you *don't want*.

To find out your values about something ask yourself the following questions:

1. 'What is most important to me about X?'
2. 'How do I know when I have X?'
3. 'What is the next most important thing about X?'
4. 'What else is important to me about X?'

The answers you generate are your values.

Values for your whole life

What are your values?

Think about beginning your life from scratch. Ask yourself:

'If I were to begin my life right now, what would I want?' 'What is important to me?' 'How do I want to live my life from now on?' 'Why?' 'Of all the people I know, who is really important to me?' 'If I had total choice in how I spent my time, where would I focus my energy?' 'What kind of work and social life do I want?'

Do a review of the major events and choices you have made in your life. Think of a time when you did something that seemed and felt totally right (some people use the phrase 'in the flow'). Ask yourself:

'Would I make the same choices again?' If yes: 'What was important about this choice to me?' If no: 'What was important?' 'What was it about it that made it right?' 'What was present? What was absent?'

A third way of discovering your values is to go out into the future several years from now and from there to look back at yourself in the present time. You would be able to notice everything you have now that is really important to you from your vantage point of the future. Ask yourself:

'What would you want to have spent your time doing?' 'Who would you have wanted to spend your time with?'

Key values

Once you have identified what is important to you, imagine if you had to live life without it. Does it really matter? If you feel you could, it is probably not a major value.

Memories

A memory is a stored representation of something you have experienced. It is your perception of what happened at the time. Everybody's memory of an event will be different because the event will be distorted, deleted and generalized according to each person's model of the world.

must know

Memories are your perception of events. But the map is not the territory.

Memories as filters

Memories themselves also act as filters of our experience. By altering our perceptions they change our experience of what comes in through our senses in the present. For example, suppose when you were small your parents divorced after a big argument. Later in life you find your memories of what you witnessed act as a filter – you have difficulty in relationships as soon as there is conflict, because you are terrified that if you have an argument it will trigger the end of the relationship. In fact, there may have been many other factors that caused your parents' divorce, but that single emotional experience has been linked in your mind with the idea of relationship breakup.

To take another example, when you were a baby a spider climbed onto your hand. You were frightened at the time and now as a grown-up you find you are afraid of insects, though you can never explain why to people. The incident has long passed out of your conscious awareness, but the memory still acts as a filter.

With NLP techniques you can address these kind of limitations on your current behaviour, even if your memories are way back in your childhood. See *Removing blocks*, pages 139–57, for ways to resolve different issues.

must know

Memories can still guide your current life, even though you may not realize consciously what is happening.

Meta programmes

The final set of internal filters we have are known as *Meta programmes*. These are deep unconscious filters that influence personal and work behaviour.

Motivation

Do you habitually move *towards* what you want in life, or *away from* what you don't want? To find out what your habitual way of doing things is, ask yourself the question: 'What do I want out of work?' Is your reply to this question mainly things you want to have or to be at work, or things you want to avoid? Are you mainly:

❑ towards
❑ towards with some away from
❑ equally towards and away from
❑ away from with some towards
❑ away from

Reason

This looks at whether you are motivated because you feel you have to do something or because it gives you possibilities.

Ask yourself these questions to find out which you are: 'Why am I choosing to do what I am doing in my work life? Is it because it gives me choices or possibilities or is it because of a sense of obligation?' Are your answers to this question mainly:

❑ necessity   ❑ possibilities   ❑ a mixture of both

Action and reflection

Are you an active or a reflective person? Active people jump in and get on with things as quickly as possible. They like to get started without spending too much time thinking about what they are doing. At the other end of the scale, reflective people prefer to spend time thinking things through in as much detail as possible before they start.

Two questions to ask yourself are: 'If I had a project to do, would I leap in straightaway and get started on it? Or would I wait first and think it through before acting?' Decide, are you:

❑ active   ❑ reflective   ❑ both

Frame of reference

What is your frame of reference for knowing something? Do you just
know inside or do you need to have some sort of external check – for
example, to talk to someone and ask his opinion? The questions to ask
are: 'How do I know whether I have done a good job? Do I just know?
Do I need someone to tell me? Is it a mixture of both?' Your answer
determines whether you are:

❑ internal   ❑ external with an internal check
❑ internal with an external   ❑ external check

Primary interest filter

What is your main focus in life, your primary interest? Are you
interested in:

❑ people   ❑ activities
❑ things   ❑ information/learning
❑ places

The questions that will determine this are: 'What makes a really happy
experience for me? The people I am spending time with? The things
around me? The place I am in? The activities I am doing? The
learning/information I am gaining?'

Relationship filter

Each of us has a different way of noticing similarity and difference. Some
people notice the similarities between things. Some people notice the
differences. People who notice sameness (match) like their jobs
and relationships to remain the same. They generally are happy to stay
in the same job for more than five years before they need to seek out
change. 'Sameness with difference' people like more change – after
about three to five years. 'Difference with exceptions' people need
greater variety – after about 18 months to three years. 'Difference'
people (mismatchers) need a lot of the new in their lives and will seek
out change and variety.

Other questions you can ask to find out sameness or difference is:
'How long do I usually stay in a particular work situation?' 'When I start
a new relationship, do I notice the differences first or the similarities?'

BIG PICTURE OR SPECIFIC

HOW WOULD YOU DESCRIBE WHAT YOU SEE THROUGH THE WINDOW?

Big picture or specific

Are you a big picture or a detail thinker? Do you enjoy thinking in abstract terms or prefer being specific? Some people have the ability to move from the detailed to the big picture and back again. This amount of flexibility can make you highly successful in the business world, where only being able to be either specific or big picture would be very limiting.

'If I were working on a new project, how much detail would I need to know? How about when I am describing my vision of the future? Do I talk first about the details or the big picture?' Notice whether you are:

- ❏ big picture
- ❏ specific
- ❏ big picture to specific
- ❏ specific to big picture

RELATIONSHIP FILTER

HOW DO YOU SEE THE RELATIONSHIP BETWEEN THESE STAMPS?

must know

When you ask
questions,
always make
sure you build
rapport (see
pages 70-77).

Convincer

What does it take to convince you about something? For some of us it
takes a number of times of hearing/seeing/doing/reading something.
Others may need to have the same evidence in front of them, or
different examples relating to the same subject, *a number of times*. A
very common number is three, which is why you often see advertisers
repeating an advertisement on television more than once in a short
time. Alternatively, your convincer might be that you need to
see/hear/do/read something *over a period of time*.

Some people *automatically* become convinced the first time
they see/hear/do/read something. Others will need to have the
same data in the same way each time. They have what is called a
consistent convincer.

Questions to ask yourself are: 'How long does it take me to become
convinced by a choice? How many times?' 'Do I know that I am good at
my job automatically? Do I have to be consistently convinced? Does it
take a period of time?' Is your convincer:

- ❏ automatic
- ❏ under three times
- ❏ over three times
- ❏ a period of weeks
- ❏ a period of months
- ❏ consistent

Thinking and feeling

Do you get very caught up in your feelings or are you able to step
outside yourself and dissociate yourself from them? Or do you go
between letting your feelings take over and being much more
thoughtful and less feeling-driven? Questions to ask yourself are:
'When I have been in a situation that I found challenging, was I caught
up in my emotions about it? Did I immediately dissociate from my
feelings? Or was it a combination of the two?' Are you:

- ❏ feeling
- ❏ thinking
- ❏ moving between the two

Time

Have you ever met someone who appeared to be totally unaware of time? Are you that person? You live life so in the moment that you are often very late or very early for appointments. You often don't wear a watch and are reluctant to put too much in your diary too far ahead. We call this way of living *in* the moment as being *in time*.

Other people are always aware of time. They are on time for appointments and they schedule their diaries and like to have their life mapped out in advance. This is called being *through time*.

Questions to ask are: 'Do I plan my time ahead, even on holiday? Do I like filling up my diary weeks ahead? If I did this, would I feel unable to live in the moment?' Are you:

❏ through time ❏ in time

must know

Becoming aware of your Meta programmes will help you understand how you live your life.

Self or others

Where is your focus? Is it on yourself or on other people? During a typical day pay attention to where your attention goes. The amount of focus you have on other *people* may well determine the type of job you do. People who usually work well in the service industry are likely to have a strong interest in other people. If you prefer to work in an area where you don't have to think about other people's needs, you are more self-oriented. Are you:

❏ self ❏ others

Decision-making

Decisions are normally made through a series of steps. You may need to see something before you can make a decision, or hear about it or even do something first. The question to ask is: 'How do I know whether a product is any good?' Do you need to:

❏ see ❏ hear ❏ do ❏ read

4 Forming relationships

If each person has a different way of thinking about the world, then how do you learn to communicate effectively with other people? In this chapter, you will learn the secrets of building instant rapport with anyone. Rapport is the basis for good communication and good relationships.

Constant communication

Communication is a constant flow of information between two people. You can't flick a switch halfway through the conversation and stop the flow. Whether you are talking to someone who is in front of you or at the other end of a telephone, you are sending each other messages about who you are and what kind of relationship you want with each other.

Filtering your first impressions

The moment you meet somebody he will begin to form an impression of you, whether you are speaking to that person or not. The instant he is aware of you or you are aware of him you are communicating.

Some of our first impressions come through what we hear another person *saying*. Many more come from what we see that person *doing* and *what he looks like*. Along with all our other impressions of the world, our first impressions are filtered through our representational systems.

Like and dislike

Have you ever walked into a room, met somebody for the first time and decided within seconds that you liked him? Or maybe you once met somebody you took an instant dislike to? Perhaps you shook that person's hand and he had an over-strong or weak handshake. Maybe he didn't look straight at you when you were speaking.

If you decided that you like a person, you probably didn't think too much about why, you just noticed how easy it was to speak to him. Whatever it was that made you like or dislike a person, it probably happened within a few seconds and was unconscious.

We like people who are like us

It is a natural reaction to like people who seem to think like we do. At a party it is likely that you will gravitate automatically to people with whom you have things in common. Maybe they like doing the same things, they went to the same university, they have children the same age, they come from the same town, they have similar interests, hobbies, politics or friends, or they are the same race, age or gender.

Charisma

However, there are charismatic people whom everyone seems to like and who are very good at getting on with a wide variety of people, even if they don't seem to have much in common with them in terms of background or interests.

What is happening here?

These people have an amazing flexibility in creating rapport very quickly with almost anyone. You can learn how to do it too.

COMMUNICATION IS CONSTANT AND 2-WAY

Rapport

Rapport is the ability to create a feeling of deep similarity and connection with another person. When you are in rapport with someone you both feel as though you are on the same wavelength. Where there is rapport there is integrity, caring and trust. When the other person talks to you, he feels a sense of comfort and understanding coming from you.

First steps to rapport

Having rapport not only helps you to get on with other people but also to communicate with them at a very deep level. Because they feel you are like them, they feel at ease with you and are prepared to open up to you. How can you build rapport? First you will need to look at how you are communicating with others.

How are you communicating?

Start by breaking down your communication into its verbal and non-verbal elements:

1. *Words:* The words and phrases you use can say a lot about you: your nationality, your culture, age, gender and class, interests, values, beliefs and the kind of work you do.

2. *Physiology:* Your non-verbal communication can show what emotions you are feeling, status yourself perceived, the power you have in relation to the other person and whether you are sexually attracted to them. Your posture, expressions and gestures all *leak* information whether or not you try to control them.

3. *Voice:* The next time someone phones you, pay attention to that person's voice. How does it sound? We say a lot with our voice tone, speed, pitch and timbre (smoothness or roughness of the voice).

Tone of voice

Try reading this statement in different ways. First read it flat. Then let your voice rise at the end of the sentence. Then let your voice go down at the end of the sentence. How does it make you sound?

▶ 'Fetch me that book?' (voice flat)

▶ 'Fetch me that book?' (voice down)

▶ 'Fetch me that book?' (voice up)

The first statement will be a fairly neutral request, the second will be a command and the third a question. Yet the words have remained the same – all that has changed has been the tone of voice.

did you know?

▶ Only 7% of your communication is through the words that you use: the content of your communication

▶ 38% is conveyed though the qualities of your voice: its tone, volume, speed and pitch

▶ 55% is through your posture, movements, gestures, facial expressions, breathing and skin-colour changes.*

*Ray L. Birdwhistell, *Kinesics and Context*, University of Pennsylvania Press, 1970

MEANS OF COMMUNICATION

7% WORDS

55% BODY (PHYSIOLOGY)

38% VOICE

Calibration

To notice the effect you are having on the person you are communicating with is called *to calibrate or to have sensory acuity* in NLP. It is your ability to notice with great precision and accuracy what is going on.

How to calibrate

The best way to calibrate is to observe the other person. Calibration means non-judgemental observation of the tiny minute-by-minute changes in someone's voice and body. Sit or stand at a 90° angle in relation to the other person so that you can observe what that person is doing with his body. At the same time, you can hear what he is saying (the words and language), as well as listen to his voice characteristics. You will find it is easier to see what is going on at this angle than if you are directly opposite the person. If you are opposite him, it will look as though you are staring at him while you are talking, and this is likely to make him feel uncomfortable – not a good way to build rapport!

When you are calibrating another person, be aware that a form of behaviour that means something to you in a certain situation does not always mean the same to someone else. Look for repeated non-verbal clues.

Calibrating another person

Observe shifts in the other person's:
❑ *Breathing:* Look for the rate and location. Is it fast or slow? Where is he breathing from? The chest or stomach?
❑ *Skin colour:* What does his skin look like? Has it become lighter or darker? Shiny or non-shiny?
❑ *Mouth*: Sometimes the lower lip size will look bigger or smaller than normal
❑ *Eyes:* How is their focus changing? Are the pupils dilating or expanding?
❑ *Face:* Have the muscles in the face slackened or tightened to make the face look more asymmetrical or symmetrical?
❑ *Voice:* Note any changes in the tone, tempo or sound (timbre) of the voice. Is the person speaking more quickly, slowly, louder, softer, or is the voice clearer or more broken up?

Matching and mirroring

Matching or mirroring another person's communication is the way to build rapport by becoming like the other person at a deep unconscious level.

Signs of rapport

When two people are in rapport they naturally match some of each other's words, as well as the postures, gestures, expressions and voice tone and speed. If you have ever seen a pair of close friends or a happy couple in love, you will have noticed that they tend to copy each other's little non-verbal habits and speak the same language – picking up ways of saying words or phrases. They also make a lot of eye contact.

Their body language is also in synch. If one person has his legs crossed, the other does. If one gestures in a particular way when talking, the other will tend to gesture with the same movements when he talks. They are not mimicking each other, but they have unconsciously got into rhythm with each other.

Next time you are in a coffee shop or restaurant, look around you. Which couples or groups of people are in rapport with each other?

MATCHING

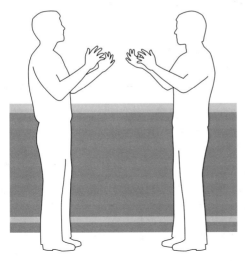

Deliberate matching and mirroring

When rapport has not happened automatically, build it by matching and mirroring another person consciously. Matching or mirroring is not the same as mimicry. When you mimic someone, you copy everything about them blindly. He will become conscious of this and probably be angry.

Calibrate the person and then match a few key things he is doing with his verbal and non-verbal communication. You don't have to match every gesture indiscriminately or in an exaggerated way – just choose a few key movements and be subtle. Get into his body/voice's rhythm. If you are successful, what you do will be outside his conscious awareness. You will know if you are successfully matching someone as you will soon feel good feelings towards him. These feelings show that you have gained a rapport and harmony with the other person.

What to match

One of the easiest things to copy is the angle at which someone holds his spine or general stance and posture. Observe how fast the other person is blinking and change your blinking to be in tune with his. Notice also how the person breathes when talking. He might be breathing deeply from the lowest part of his abdomen, from the middle of his chest or high up in his chest. If you match how someone breathes, it makes your body go into a similar position to his. It also helps you to talk at the same pitch and speed. Breathing deeply makes you speak more slowly and deeply. Breathing from higher in the body makes you speak more quickly and at a higher pitch.

Matching voice qualities

There are many situations in which we don't have the opportunity to meet another person face to face, but have to talk to him over the telephone. Unfortunately when you are talking to someone over the telephone you will not be able to use your skills of matching and mirroring body language. But the other person will still form an impression of you in just a few seconds.

As soon as you hear the person you are talking to, you can match his voice qualities as well as the words he marks out by tone or emphasis in his sentences, and other linguistic idiosyncrasies such as his sentence length or particular phrases.

Each person you meet will also have a few words and phrases that he marks out in his speech by using them time and time again or by putting particular emphasis on them. This is language that has some personal meaning or emotional or cultural significance for the person. Use these words and you will sound like him. An example is the jargon that different professions use. Families and groups of friends also have a shared vocabulary.

Cross-cultural communication

The speed or pace at which people speak varies considerably according to various factors, including their preferred representational system (see pages 36–37) and mood, culture or nationality. For example, if you have a telephone conversation with a businessman from the country, he may talk much more slowly and softly than a businesswoman from a fast-paced city.

To keep rapport with someone, it is vital to talk at a similar pace and volume. If you speak too quickly or loudly or too slowly and softly, you will lose his interest and you might even begin to irritate each other. It is also important to copy voice timbre. Timbre is the quality of the voice. Notice whether the other person speaks in a clear and resonant voice or with a gravelly, harsh timbre. What is your own voice like? Can you change it?

Markers of rapport

Match but don't mimic the other person. What you are doing should remain outside the person's conscious awareness. As the two of you get into rapport, you might notice a warm feeling, probably in your stomach. The other person's face and neck may change colour slightly. This is known as a *colour shift*. You may suddenly feel close to him, as if you have known them for a long time. It's likely that the other person will feel this if you are in rapport.

Crossover mirroring

Crossover mirroring is a very subtle way of further developing the skills of matching and mirroring the other person. It is useful if someone is angry or is in an agitated state for example and you want to keep rapport with that person but not go into the same state as him. With crossover mirroring, instead of matching several things the other person is doing with his body and voice, you copy the form of one gesture with another part of your body. For example, you can mirror someone's *pace* of breathing by beating out the same pace with a pencil or tapping it out with your finger.

Pacing and leading

In NLP, building rapport with others is known as *pacing and leading*. *Pacing* is the skill you use to match the other person in order to build rapport. *Leading* is when you lead them into another state.

Pacing

Suppose you are feeling very happy one day. Suddenly the phone rings. It is a friend who is in a totally different mood because he has just had his wallet stolen. How do you keep rapport while not bringing your own mood down? First show empathy through matching some of his key words or voice qualities. If he is talking slowly, then do the same. If he is angry, raise your voice a little. Trying to calm the person by using the opposite kind of voice will just annoy them more. He is likely to feel that you haven't *got* what he was saying.

must know

Four keys to rapport

1. Calibrate the other person – observe their physiology, position, movements and breathing, blinking, voice, words.
2. Watch your own communication, physiology, voice and words.
3. Pace the other person.
4. Lead the other person.

Leading

After you have *paced* a person and shown him you are on his side, you can begin to do what is known as *leading*. To lead someone, you keep rapport while gradually changing the speed at which you are talking, or shifting your position slightly so that he follows you. When he follows you he will be changing his emotional state.

Mismatching

When two people aren't in rapport and are not getting along, they *mismatch* each other. This means that they do not match or mirror non-verbal communication or voice or speech. They are out of synch and feel disconnected from each other.

Examples of mismatching

When two people are mismatching each other, one person might be speaking slowly while the other person is speaking loudly and quickly. Perhaps a group of people is talking together at the bar, but one person in the group is mismatching the others, leaning back in his chair and looking at the door rather than at his friends.

Deliberately mismatching

There are times you may want to deliberately break rapport and mismatch. Why would you want to do this? It may not be appropriate for you to be in rapport with someone, for example a person who is trying to manipulate you or does not generally have your best interests at heart.

If you are in a conversation and you want to break rapport, shift your position so that you break the state you are both in. You can do this very quickly and easily by just looking away or stepping back or turning away. The conversation will suddenly shift and you have the opportunity to end it with a few words if you wish.

MISMATCHING

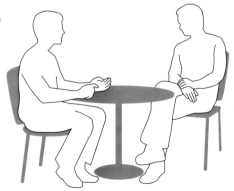

5 Creating achievable outcomes

What makes some people more successful than others? What makes a tennis champion or a top business person? Consistent high achievers are outcome focused – they decide what they want, they are motivated and they take action to get it.

What do you want?

This is the all-important first question! In NLP, it is answered by setting an outcome. The word 'outcome' is used in NLP as a statement about a desired state that you want instead of the present state you are in. It is a clear statement and representation in your mind of what you want.

---

must know

An outcome contains a commitment that a wish does not.

Improving your life

How do you know whether your life could be improved by setting some outcomes? Consider the following questions:

- ❏ Do you know where you are going?
- ❏ Have you achieved what you want in your professional career?
- ❏ Do you have the relationships you want?
- ❏ Do you have the friendships you want?
- ❏ Do you have the balance you want between your work and personal life?

If you can't answer all of these questions with a clear 'yes', then you could probably introduce some more focus and clear outcomes into your life to get what you want.

Make your 'wants' into outcomes

One way to start thinking about the outcomes that would be appropriate for you is to list your wants and wishes. What do you want? The first step to anything is to wish for it. But the next step is to make an outcome. This will begin the process of focusing your thoughts *away from* any present dissatisfaction and problems and *towards* what you want as a final goal.

If you find it difficult to say what you want, it may be because:

☐ You think you shouldn't or can't have what you want in your life.

☐ You are used to being more focused on the past or present than the future.

☐ You are afraid to voice it.

☐ You think you will lose too much in another area by having it.

☐ You think it is impossible to get.

☐ You are used to thinking about what other people want rather than what you want.

If you answer 'yes' to any of these questions, you may be hampered by unconscious beliefs. List your beliefs about yourself and use the belief change techniques later in the book to make changes that will free up your thinking.

Outcomes set a direction

An outcome may just refer to the result you want to get from taking a specific action, for example the outcome of doing a technique, or it may refer to the big outcome you want for an area of your life or your life as a whole.

Whatever your outcome, it sets a direction for you – it is what you intend to focus your energies and actions on from now on. Always start with the destination in mind. When you know your outcome then you can begin to plot out a journey from your present position to that place. You won't always have all the knowledge that will take you there, but you will have enough of a picture to take some first steps and the others will follow on as you continue on the journey.

> **must know**
>
> An outcome is a statement that says what you want. An outcome takes account of:
> Where you are now – your *present state*.
> What you want – your *desired state*.

Big visions

The highly successful people that NLP has modelled all have one thing in common – they have inspiring, motivating visions that pull them forward and make them overcome any problems, blocks or obstacles they encounter on the way to their goal.

must know

Focus, action, persistence
The secret of success in life is:
▶ first to focus
▶ then to take action
▶ and finally to be persistent

A believable vision

A motivating vision will need to be as large as you can make it if it is really going to be successful in inspiring you and other people at the same time. However your vision doesn't need to be probable. It just needs to be believable and possible for you to be able to achieve it. For example, you might want to expand your business, and with the help of your employees it will be possible but everyone will need to work hard to achieve it. Without hard work the expansion won't succeed.

Outcome-based thinking versus problem-based thinking

When you consistently think in terms of outcomes in the different areas of your life, this is known as *outcome thinking* or *having an outcome orientation*. Outcome-based thinking asks questions such as: 'What do I want and what steps can I take to get it?' 'If this is the problem, what do I want instead and what steps can I take to get it?'

When you are focused on your present position (state) and your current problems it is known as *problem thinking*. Problem-based thinking is blame based and will ask questions such as: 'What is the problem?' 'Who's responsible for causing it?' 'Who's to blame?'

The world is full of people who go through life focused on problems rather than visions. Problem-based thinking will keep you stuck in the problem. Outcome-based thinking will move you forward.

Well-formed outcomes

In order to make a general goal into a compelling outcome it needs to be made sharp and focussed. With what is called a *well-formed outcome*, you have a very clear image of what it will be like when you have made that change in your life.

This will make it motivating enough to make you want to move out of your present position (present state) to your outcome (desired state). It will also inspire you to take action and encourage you to face any resistance along the way.

How do you know when an outcome is well formed?

❏ It is stated in positive language.

❏ You have stated evidence for how you will know when you have it – you know how it will look, feel and sound when you have it.

❏ It is specific and is set in a context – i.e. you know where and when you want it.

❏ You can carry out the actions necessary to get the outcome – you are responsible for achieving it.

❏ It is good for you and for your life as a whole.

A study in an American university asked undergraduates in their first year whether they had written down their goals. Around 5% had. Twenty years later, the same researchers came back to the undergraduates and discovered that the 5% who had written down their goals were worth more than the other 95% put together on a purely fiscal basis. And those 5% held more positions of power and influence in industry, business and government than the other 95%.

Outcomes: coaching another person

If you are coaching another person, always make sure that you spend adequate time finding out his outcomes.

First make sure that the person comes up with the outcomes that are personally important to him. The clearer the person is about what he really wants, the easier it will be to work out what techniques and tools will create the change he wants. Here are a few pointers to bear in mind:

▶ Get clear on what the person would like to have achieved by the end of the time you have together.

▶ Find out what overall vision he has for his future and how the outcomes fit into it. The bigger and more specific the person's vision, the easier it will be to come up with a set of goals with different end dates to support that vision.

▶ Use your observation skills to really notice which of the person's outcomes are particularly important to him. He may not always want to state these straightaway, but clues in his body language or emotionally charged words when he talks about them will help to alert you.

must know

When you hear someone use the word 'try', they already have a picture in their mind of something not succeeding. When you hear them use the word 'will', they have a picture in their mind of what success will look like and they are determined to take steps to achieve it.

'Try' and 'will'

'I will try to pick up that pen from the table.'

'I will pick up the pen from the table.'

What is the difference between the two sentences above? The first sentence assumes there is the possibility of failure, while the second sentence assumes there will be success. A well-formed outcome will always focus on success without letting the possibility of failure get in the way.

Outcome questions

Each time you have an outcome, run it through these questions to make sure that it is well formed and therefore easily realizable.

What do I want?

Outcome: positive and specific statement

Because what you focus on is what you get, make sure you use positive language to state your outcomes. If you always know what you *don't* want and are never clear what you *do* want, you will end up with what you don't want.

Positive language does not mean that you have to feel positive when you think of the outcome. It simply means focusing on what you want rather than what you don't want, for example 'I want a new car' rather than 'I don't want my beaten-up old car.' Remember that every time you say to yourself 'I don't want something in my life' what you are doing is focusing on that thing. That's why you will end up with what you were trying to avoid. If your main motivation in deciding on an outcome is to *move away* from a current situation or problem, ask yourself: 'What do I want *instead*?

> **must know**
>
> Say it the way you want it,
> Turn 'I don't want a green bus'
> into ' I want a red bus.'

Be as specific as you can

Imagine you want to go on a trip to the USA. You choose to fly from London, but do not specify a US city. If you ended up in New York or California, would it make a difference? Of course it would. You wouldn't dream of doing that, so treat your outcome as a specific destination too. For example, suppose you want more money. Write down how much you want *specifically*. 'More' could mean 'a few pennies extra' or 'an extra million'.

> **must know**
>
> Outcomes are always most
> effective if you write them
> down. This will allow you to
> hone in on what you want
> with precision.

watch out!

Avoid the question 'Why?'
In problem-based thinking,
people ask questions such as
'Why do I have this problem?'
'Who is to blame for it?'
These questions just get you
stuck in self-blame and take
your energy away from
thinking about what you want
instead. Change your questions
round quickly to focus on what
you want instead.

Write your outcome in the present tense.
Instead of saying, 'My goal is to have an annual salary of £1,000,000 by 20th August 2020,' you should express the goal as 'It is 20th August 2020 and I have an annual salary of £1,000,000.' The brain processes a goal that has been written in the present tense as if it is actually a truth *now*. So you act accordingly.

Where am I now?
Present state

In order to achieve what you want, you need to move from where you are now (your present state) to your outcome (desired state). So when you write down the outcome you want, write down your starting point as well. This means that you will be able to measure your progress accurately along the way and see how far you have moved away from your starting point and towards your finishing point.

Are there aspects of your current situation that you need to ensure are preserved in any outcomes you set? What do you want to change in your life and what is it that you want to stay the same?

How will I know when I have it?
Evidence

A well-formed outcome needs an evidence procedure. You need evidence for two reasons:

1. So that you know you have got the outcome. How will you know that you have got what you want?

2. So that you know when you are on track to get it and when you have gone off track. How will you measure how near you are to it or how far away?

What will you hear, see and feel when you have your outcome?
Think about what your experience of getting what you want will be like when you finally achieve it. For example, when you have a fit, toned,

muscular body, what does that feel like? How about when you are earning the amount of money you want to earn? What does it feel like and look like?

Imagine you have what you want right now. Try it on. Feel what it feels like inside when you have it. What else can you feel? What can you see? What are people around you saying? What other sounds are there around you?

Mental rehearsal

Mental rehearsal is a technique that is widely used to help sportspeople improve their performance. Here's how to do it:

▶ Think about an outcome you have clarified.

▶ Imagine that you are already achieving that outcome. For example, if you want to ski down a red run, see yourself already doing it through your own eyes. Feel the snow beneath your skis. Hear the sound of your skis on the snow.

▶ As you do this, if any negative inner voices start to come up with objections as to why this won't work, notice what the purpose of this self-talk is.

▶ Can you change this self-talk? Are there any limiting beliefs or emotions to deal with?

▶ Repeat making the pictures. Practice makes perfect.

Where, when, how and with whom?
Context

In what contexts do you want what you want? And where and when don't you want it? There may be some situations in which you want a particular goal and others in which you don't. For example, you might want a job promotion if it is in the same location as you are currently working in. However, if you had a promotion that meant moving countries, would you still want it? Ask yourself: 'Where, when and with whom do I want this outcome?' 'Where when and with whom do I not want this outcome?'

must know

When you have a big reason why you want your goal, you will find it easy to take whatever action is needed to get it.

Am I congruent about wanting this?

Being congruent in NLP means every part of you wants something. You really want it whole-heartedly. We have all made goals that look good on paper but when push comes to shove we don't really want them enough to go after them 100 per cent.

To check that you are congruent about your outcome, ask yourself:

- ❏ 'What will having this outcome add to my life?'
- ❏ 'What will it allow me to do?'
- ❏ 'How much do I really want it?'
- ❏ 'Is it absolutely right for me?'
- ❏ 'Are there any adjustments I could make so that I could be totally congruent about it?'

Another way of asking the same question is to think about what it is important to have, do or be in your life (see *What do I want?* page 85).

Is it only for me? Can I take responsibility for achieving this outcome?

Is your outcome under your control? If you need to involve other people in order to get it, how can you take responsibility for persuading them to help you? What part of your outcome can you do without other people's help?

What resources do I have now and what resources do I need to get my outcome?

Make an assessment of the resources you think you will need to meet your outcome and the relevant resources you have now.

- ❏ Where are you are right now? What are your resources in terms of:
  Mental and emotional skills: Intelligence and knowledge.
  Physical possessions: What you own, the money you have.
  People: Your family and friends and the network of people you can ask for help.
  Models: The people you don't know but can study and learn from.

- [ ] What resources can you acquire or set up?
- [ ] What can you do straightaway?
- [ ] Have you ever had or done this before? If not, do you know anyone who has? What would happen if you acted as if you had done it?
- [ ] What can you continue doing that you are already doing?

Is it good for me and my life?

The different parts of your life can not be compartmentalized – they are part of a whole. Every outcome is likely to have a knock-on effect on other parts. What effect will the outcome have on your life? Also, although we are all individuals, everything we do impacts our environment and other people. How will your outcome fit into your wider world, including those around you? Ask yourself:

- [ ] 'What will happen if I get this outcome? How will my life change? Are there any positive or negative secondary consequences that I haven't considered?'
- [ ] 'How does getting this outcome benefit me?'
- [ ] 'What changes will occur in the rest of my life? Which parts of my life do I need to set outcomes in to ensure that I retain balance between the different areas of my life?'
- [ ] 'How do I make sure I keep the parts of my current situation that I like?'
- [ ] 'What will I gain or lose if I get this outcome? How much energy and commitment is it going to take to really get it? Will I have to sacrifice anything to ensure that I reach it? Am I congruent about this?'
- [ ] 'Will it be good not only for me but also for other people in my life? My family? My friends? The community as a whole? How will it impact them?'

must know

In order for an outcome to be well formed, it has to fit into our lives as a whole. And if we want to motivate other people to help us get it, it needs to be positive for them as well.

watch out!

'What' not 'how'
The outcome questions don't ask you to come up with a whole plan for *how* to get what you want, just a first step. You don't have to know exactly *how* you are going to get what you want. You just need to get really clear on the *what*. Once you are clear on the *what*, the *how* will emerge as you focus on the first step.

What is the first step?

When you have run an outcome through these
questions, ask yourself: 'What is the first step
I can take to achieve my outcome?' You may
have the most congruent outcome and still do
nothing to get it. Decide on some steps you can
take towards getting it and the ones you can
do immediately. How big is your outcome? Can
it be broken down into several outcomes? Would that make it easier to
think of steps towards it?

Working out the first step

If you are not sure how to come up with a first step:

❏ Imagine you already have your outcome. Go to that place where you
have achieved it.

❏ Now look back at now and all the time between now and the goal you
have just achieved.

❏ What were the steps you took to reach your goal?

Once an outcome has been experienced as if it has already happened,
the brain becomes very creative. You will find you unconsciously begin to
come up with lots of ways in which to attain it.

Write steps down

Write down the steps you can think of. It may also help you if you share
your outcomes with someone you know. This may help you to commit to
action, find support and resources, and sometimes gain extra clarity.

An example of a well-formed outcome

Here is an example of a goal that has been put through the outcome
question process:

*I have increased my sales by 20% on the final day of July. The evidence is
that I am looking at the figures in front of me and saying, 'Well done.' I am
in my office. The consequences are that I can ask my employer for more
money because of my improved performance. This is a goal that is*

achievable by me. I have resources: the support of my office and the know-how. I do need extra contacts. My first step is to plan how to build my client network.

Make all your outcomes SMART

 S Specific
Simple

 M Measurable
Meaning to you

 A As if now
Achievable
All areas of your life

R Realistic
Responsible/ecological

T Timed

Outcome questions

Remember to ask yourself the outcome questions:

1. *Outcome:* 'What do you want?' Make it positive and specific and in the present tense.
2. *Present state:* 'Where are you now?' 'What is stopping you having it now?'
3. *Evidence:* 'How will you know when you have it?' 'What will you see, hear, feel, etc., when you have it?'
4. *Context:* 'Where, when, how and with whom do you want it?'
5. *Congruency:* 'Are you congruent about wanting it?' 'What will it get for you or allow you to do?'
6. *Self-initiated and self-maintained:* 'Is it only for you?' 'Can you take responsibility for achieving this outcome?'
7. *Resources:* 'What resources do you have now and what resources do you need to get your outcome?'
8. *Ecology:* 'Is it good for you and your life? What will you gain or lose if you have it?'
9. *Action:* 'What is the first step?'

The Disney method

The Disney method is a way of coming up with creative thinking around an outcome. It was modelled from Walt Disney and devised by Robert Dilts. Disney was enormously successful in coming up with big visions that came to fruition because he had the flexibility to have several points of view – those of the dreamer, the realist and the critic.

Dreamer, realist and critic

▶ The *dreamer* creates a vision for the future. He can define what he wants and the benefits of having it.

▶ The *realist* gives those ideas a tangible and concrete time frame and assesses who can carry them out.

▶ The *critic* looks at what will work and what might go wrong, and acts as a filter.

Many people are naturally able to take one of these positions when they evaluate their goals. However if you are only a dreamer, your plans will never come to fruition. If you have a dreamer and a realist in a team but no critic, you will lack an objective filter for your ideas. If you put a dreamer and a critic together with no realist, the dreamer will feel criticized and the critic will find the dreamer unrealistic. If you want to be successful in a creative endeavour, you need a little bit of all three.

Using the Disney method

Use this method when you need to come up with a creative goal or vision.

▶ Explore what you want from the dreamer's point of view. You can do this by brainstorming all of the possibilities and options and keeping them free from critique or realism at this point. Ask yourself:

'What do I want?'

'Why would I like this?'

'What are the benefits of having this happen?'

'What is the vision that will allow me to know when I have this?'

'Where do I want this idea to take me to?'

'Who do I want to be in relation to manifesting this idea?'

watch out!

It is important to do the Disney method *in order* and to give enough time to each step before proceeding to the next step.

▶ Explore what you want from the realist's point of view.

Look at what you want and turn it into a concrete and tangible plan. Ask yourself:

'When will the goal be completed?'

'Who is going to be involved in getting the goal?'

'How will I make sure it happens?' Define the first and subsequent steps.

'What will let me know that I am on your way to the goal or have moved off-course?'

'What evidence will let me know when I have reached the goal?'

▶ Explore what you want from the critic's point of view.

Check for the consequences of getting the vision. Is it ecological? What will it be like when you get it? Ask yourself:

'When and where would I *not* want to implement this plan or idea?'

'What is currently needed or missing from the plan?'

'Who will this new idea affect?'

'Who could prevent or ensure the effectiveness of the idea?'

'What do I need to know about those people and what they need? What benefits are there for them in my idea succeeding or not succeeding?'

'Why might someone find fault with my plan or vision?'

'What positive benefits are there in how I am doing things now? What have I got now? What am I now?'

'How can I keep those things when I have my goal?'

6 Your language

If you want to change the results in your life, you need to change the language you use. The Meta Model is an NLP tool you can use to gain an insight into what is going on under the surface of the words you use. The Milton Model is a tool you can use to produce deep behaviour change unconsciously.

Deep thought

The language we use inside our heads (self-talk) and in conversation gives away what pictures are running inside our head as we speak (our internal representations). This is the *linguistic* part of Neuro-Linguistic Programming.

The first stage in changing behaviour is to find out what your language is telling you about your unconscious thought processes. Then you can reprogramme your behaviour using changes in language, thinking and other techniques.

Recovering what has been deleted, generalized and distorted

Sometimes, if you are listening to someone speak, you have to suddenly stop and check inside yourself to make sense of what that person is saying. It is a clue that he may have some gap in his thinking as a result of the way he distorts the world. At that point, you need to stop and ask a question to clarify what is going on.

Questioning

As native speakers of a language we often take short cuts and leaps in language, as we know that other native speakers can generally follow our logic. However, as you well know, there is much misunderstanding between even two speakers of the same language, due to differences in thinking styles and the language they produce.

Questions can be used to clarify what one speaker assumes the other will understand. Through

must know

Two levels of language
According to linguist Noam Chomsky, there are two levels to language:
1. What we say (the surface structure)
2. The deeper level of unconscious thinking (the deep structure).

clarification the speaker can also get clearer about the unconscious assumptions he feeds into his language – and this opens up new choices for him. You can also ask questions of yourself to become more aware of your patterns.

When you are talking to somebody, always ask yourself what question will:

▶ get to the heart of the issue
▶ give the person new choices
▶ be the difference that makes a difference
▶ help them to get to their outcome

Why? Is the question you are least likely to use in NLP. The answer to a 'why' question is about reasons rather than about structure, strategy and process. It encourages blame rather than change.

What? Asks you to be specific in the information you give to the questioner. For example, 'What do you want as an outcome?' 'What happened?' 'For what purpose?'

Who? Asks you to be specific about the people involved. For example, 'Who do you want that outcome with?' 'Who was present when you felt that way?' 'Who is usually present when you behave like that?'

How? Asks you for the strategy by which you do something. For example, 'How do you behave specifically?' 'What are the steps involved?' 'How do you know when to get irritated or be happy?' Unlike 'why', 'how' only asks you for a process – which can then be reprogrammed using NLP techniques.

Where? Asks you for a context or a location. For example, 'Where do you behave like this?' 'Where do you want this outcome?'

When? This asks you to be specific about a time. For example, 'When do you do this?' 'When do you want this?' 'When will you have changed your behaviour?'

The Meta Model

John Grinder and Richard Bandler observed the questions that the therapists they modelled for NLP used to get below the surface issues their clients presented and as a result they developed a specific set of questions that is known as the Meta Model.

The Meta Model questions

The Meta Model gets to the deeper levels of language and reveals what parts of someone's experience he has deleted, generalized or distorted out of his conscious awareness. Once you know this, you can discover what is behind his behaviour. Deletion, generalization and distortion are revealed in different ways in the language we use and there are different Meta Model questions for each.

UNCOVER WHAT IS REALLY GOING ON UNDERNEATH THE SURFACE

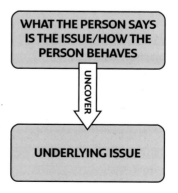

WHAT THE PERSON SAYS IS THE ISSUE/HOW THE PERSON BEHAVES

UNCOVER

UNDERLYING ISSUE

Meta Model - Deletion

1. Nominalizations

Nominalizations are verbs that have been made into nouns. The rule is, if it's a noun and you can't put it in a wheelbarrow, then it's a nominalization.

Examples of nominalization statements

❏ 'We had an understanding.'
❏ 'She values her independence.'
❏ 'He thinks freedom is the most important thing.'

Meta Model responses

These are the Meta Model questions you would ask when faced with a nominalization:

❏ 'What specifically do you understand?'
❏ 'What about being independent is important to her?'
❏ 'What is it about being free that is important to him?'

2. Unspecified verbs

Unspecified verbs are verbs where some detail of the action is not specified.

Examples of unspecified verb statements

❏ 'He rejected me.'
❏ 'He touched me.'

Meta Model responses

❏ 'How specifically did he reject you?'
❏ 'How did he touch you?'

3. Lack of referential index

Here an action is specified, but *who* is doing the action is left unspecified.

Examples of lack of referential index statements

❏ 'They stole candy from my house.'
❏ 'It's not fair.'

Meta Model responses

❏ 'Who stole candy from your house?'
❏ 'For whom is it not fair?'

4. Comparative deletions

Here a comparison is made, but what it is being compared to is unspecified.
Comparative deletions include words like 'better', 'worse', 'more', 'less', 'best', 'worst'.

Examples of comparative deletion statements

❏ 'I'm a better person.'
❏ 'She's the worst.'

Meta Model responses

❏ 'Better than whom?'
❏ 'Compared to whom?'

Meta Model - Generalization

1. Universal quantifiers

There are words like 'always', 'all', 'every', 'everyone', 'never', 'no one'.

Examples of universal quantifier statements

- ❏ 'He's always kinder to you than to me.'
- ❏ 'She never listens to what I am saying.'
- ❏ 'Everyone thinks I'm great!'

Meta Model responses

- ❏ 'He's always kinder to you?'
- ❏ 'Never? Has there ever been a time when she listened to you?'
- ❏ 'Everyone?'

2. Modal operators

A modal operator is a word that implies possibility or necessity. There are three types of modal operators:

Possibility – can, will

Impossibility – can't, won't

Necessity – must, have to, it is necessary

Examples of modal operator statements

- ❏ 'I can't do this.'
- ❏ 'I have to make the appointment.'

Meta Model responses

- ❏ 'Have you ever been able to do this?'
- ❏ 'What would happen if you didn't go?'

must know

By using these generalizations you limit your choices.

Meta Model - Distortion

1. Mind reading

This is when you make an assumption about what another person means without checking with them. This is revealed in language that implies that you know what is going on for another person emotionally or in his thinking. You 'mind read' because you impose your distorted views of how the world is onto the other person rather than recognizing that he may have very different views, values and motives. Mind reading can lead to inaccurate and often negative thoughts about other people and can therefore be harmful to relationships.

Examples of mind-reading statements: 'He doesn't like me,' 'She is doing that deliberately to hurt me,' 'He loves me,' 'They are not interested in being my friends.'

Meta Model responses

There are two ways to respond to mind reading. First of all, you can ask the other person what he is thinking. If that is not possible, ask for some more sensory-based information – collect some evidence to test what you believe to be true: 'How do you know? What leads you to believe that is true?' 'How do you know he doesn't like you?' 'How do you know she is doing that deliberately to hurt you?' 'How do you know he loves you?'

2. Reversed or projected mind reading

Mind reading can work two ways. The first is where you assume you know what the other person is thinking, as in the examples above. The second way is where you assume that the other person will, or should, know what *you* are thinking. You project onto the other person your expectations about what he should be able to understand.

Examples of reversed mind-reading statements: 'He should know what I like,' 'I can tell they hate me,' 'I know what's good for my own son,' 'You ought to know how I feel.'

Meta Model responses

Answer by challenging the evidence: 'How should he know what you like?' 'How can you tell they hate you?' 'What leads you to believe that you know what's good for your own son?'

must know

Meta Model
distortion
▶ mind reading
▶ reversed/
projected mind
reading
▶ lost
performative
▶ cause and effect
▶ complex
equivalence
▶ presuppositions

3. Lost performative

A *lost performative* is a value judgement where the evidence on which the judgement has been based has been left out of what is said. Lost performatives are expressed in the form of generalized standards or rules about the world. Who has set these standards is not mentioned.

Examples of lost performative statements

- ❏ 'It's bad to be late.'
- ❏ 'That is a stupid idea.'
- ❏ 'It is not important to pay attention to the details of life.'
- ❏ 'Obviously it is the right way to do it.'
- ❏ 'Clearly that is the meaning.'

Meta Model responses

- ❏ 'Who says it's bad to be late? According to whom is it bad to be late?'
- ❏ 'How do you know it's stupid? According to whom?'
- ❏ 'Who says it is not important to pay attention to the details of life?'
- ❏ 'Who says it is the right way to do it?'
- ❏ 'How do you know that is the meaning?'

To avoid making lost performative statements, be precise in your judgement and own what you say. This keeps you away from sweeping generalizations and 'truths' that are actually distortions. Make 'I' statements, for example:

- ❏ 'I believe that...'
- ❏ 'I think...'
- ❏ 'My opinion is...'
- ❏ 'My judgement is...'

4. Cause and effect

A cause and effect statement implies that A causes B – that one person's action, communication or behaviour can directly cause a response in another person. It therefore implies there is a lack of choice.

This kind of thinking can cause a lot of pain within relationships. If you feel that you have no choice but to respond in a certain way every time you encounter certain behaviour, or hear a certain tone of voice, or see a certain facial expression, you are putting severe limitations on your own life. In effect, you relinquish all responsibility for controlling your own emotional state, because you 'have' to have that reaction.

Examples of cause and effect statements

❑ 'If he leaves me, I will get depressed.'

❑ 'When he shouts at me, I will get angry.'

Meta Model responses

Responding to cause and effect statements by asking for a counter-example – an exception – that disproves the general rule that has been invented.

❑ 'How would him leaving you cause you not to get depressed?'

❑ 'Has he ever shouted at you and you not got angry?'

5. Complex equivalence

This is a statement that implies that A is equivalent to B.

Examples of complex-equivalence statements

❑ 'His being late means he doesn't like me.'

❑ 'I know he's angry because he gave me that look.'

Meta Model responses

❑ 'How does his being late mean he doesn't like you?'

❑ 'How does his giving you that look mean he's angry?'

6. Presuppositions

Presuppositions are statements that assume that something is true or will be true.

Examples of presupposition statements

❑ 'I'm concerned that my new boss will be as difficult about regulations as the last one.' (The presupposition is that the last boss was difficult.)

Meta Model responses

❑ 'How specifically was your previous boss difficult?'

The Milton Model

The Milton Model is a breakdown of the language that the hypnotherapist Milton Erickson used with his patients to get them to change their patterns of behaviour. The Milton Model is a way of using language to talk to the unconscious mind of another person.

must know

All change is unconscious. You notice the behaviour change consciously but it is your unconscious mind that constructs and carries out new ways of making that behaviour happen. The Milton Model is a way of giving new instructions to the unconscious mind.

The Meta Model versus the Milton Model

Unlike the Meta Model, which is a series of questions that are designed to get someone to be specific, clear and precise, the Milton Model contains a series of phrases and patterns of language that are almost the opposite. They include generalizations, ambiguous statements and indirect language.

While the Meta Model encourages you to become clear about what you have deleted, generalized and distorted so that you can communicate more efficiently with other people, the Milton Model language patterns are general or indirectly suggestive. They actually have the effect of making the person hearing them go inside himself and use his creative imagination.

In the Milton Model, the person goes into an altered state in which the conscious mind is distracted, leaving the unconscious mind free to listen to the language of the therapist. His unconscious mind interprets the Milton Model language as an instruction to access new resources and produce new ways of doing things. The Milton

Model leaves the choice of *how* the other person does that up to them by keeping the instructions deliberately vague. This allows the person to dig deep into his unconscious resources to produce change easily and effortlessly.

Milton Model and trance

Another way of thinking about the differences between the Meta Model and the Milton Model is to think about a trance. Sometimes you want a person to be in a trance – a state in which that person can access his unconscious resources and make leaps of imagination. In that case, you should use the Milton Model.

On the other hand, taking someone out of his over-real personal world can be like getting him out of a hypnotic trance – so in this situation you will need to ask the person specific questions by using the Meta Model.

The differences between the Meta Model and the Milton Model

Milton	Meta
Is general and vague.	Is precise and specific.
Accesses resources at an unconscious level.	Brings resources into conscious awareness.
Uses deletions, distortions and generalization to bring about trance.	Challenges deletions, distortions and generalization to break a trance.
Uses suggestions to produce behavioural change.	Asks questions to uncover what's going on underneath the surface language to produce behavioural change.
Produces a trans-derivational search. The listener comes up with their own new meanings.	

Trance

The Milton Model provides a list of very effective language patterns that have a semi-hypnotic effect. In other words, they are heard by the unconscious mind in such a way as to produce a trance.

What is a trance?

The idea of trance is much misunderstood, mainly because of the images we have from Svengali-like figures in films and from stage hypnosis. A trance is simply a relaxed state in which it becomes easier to communicate with the unconscious mind and to access its resources. Hypnosis is a means by which you can get yourself into that relaxed state. You can be directed into a trance state by another person or do it yourself.

Types of trance

Natural trance

Trance is a natural state of relaxation. Every day there are probably several occasions when you go into a light trance – for example, driving, getting up in the morning, cooking, writing on the computer or eating. When in a trance you lose time or experience time happening more quickly or slowly than normal.

Shock/injury trance

There are other types of trances too. For example, if you have an accident and go into shock, you may not notice some of the details first of all. Some people don't notice even severe injuries for a while afterwards. There have been cases in marathon running where the runner has been in such a trance that he hasn't noticed the pain of a broken leg, for example.

Negative trance

When you get caught up in thinking obsessively about something you are anxious about and you go round and round in your head and can't find a

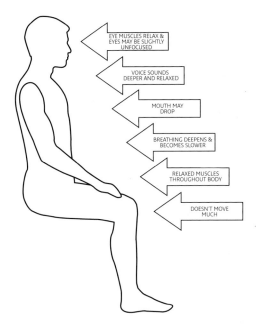

EYE MUSCLES RELAX &
EYES MAY BE SLIGHTLY
UNFOCUSED

VOICE SOUNDS
DEEPER AND RELAXED

MOUTH MAY
DROP

BREATHING DEEPENS &
BECOMES SLOWER

RELAXED MUSCLES
THROUGHOUT BODY

DOESN'T MOVE
MUCH

solution to the issue, you have created a *negative trance*. You feel stuck in your own thinking and your imagination is taking you deeper and deeper into your own negative thoughts and feelings. Certain triggers may take you into this trance as a matter of habit. These triggers are known as *anchors* (see pages 130–37).

Hypnotic trance

A hypnotic trance is simply a deliberately induced positive trance. Just like an everyday trance, it is a pleasant state of relaxation in which time may be distorted.

Indicators of trance

As well as time distortion, other indicators of trances of different depths are:

❏ relaxed muscles throughout body
❏ minimal movement
❏ the voice sounds relaxed and deeper

- ❏ the mouth may drop
- ❏ the eye muscles relax and the eyes may be slightly unfocused
- ❏ the breathing deepens and becomes slower
- ❏ amnesia – where a person forgets what they have experienced while in trance
- ❏ catalepsy – when the body becomes so still that it can stay in the same position for a long period of time
- ❏ hallucination – when a person imagines seeing something that isn't there or doesn't see something that is there
- ❏ anaesthesia – where a person doesn't feel pain. That's why you see people having pins stuck into their hands sometimes in stage hypnosis acts

Language and trance

Hypnotherapists use language to direct another person to go into a trance. Some hypnotists write scripts to use for anything from helping their clients to stop smoking to stress relief. Many of these use very direct, authoritarian language to tell the other person to go into a trance.

Erickson was different. He didn't use scripts and his language was permissive and indirect and included metaphors and stories. He used a variety of approaches depending on the needs of his clients. This meant that he took account of what type of people they were and so he bypassed any resistance that they might have had to therapy by being very flexible in his communication.

He was particularly attuned to non-verbal communication and could observe the smallest changes in the patient's physiology. This alerted him to what effect his words were having.

Milton Model language

Use these phrases to take another person into an altered state where he can access his inner resources and produce changes.

Milton Model - deletion

Deletion

1. Comparative deletions

Here a comparison is made but it is not specified what the comparison is in relation to. This deletion allows the other person to choose whatever information he wants to put as the 'what' or 'who' the comparison is about, for example:

'It feels more or less the right time...'

2. Lack of referential index

This is a phrase that is vague enough not to make a reference to anything specifically in the person's experience. As it remains general, it enables him to interpret it with some meaning appropriate to him, for example:

'There are things around you that are important to you.'

3. Lost performative

This is basically a statement that includes a judgement but where anything about who is making the judgement, or why, is left out, for example:

'And it's really great to remember all the things you do well...'

Milton Model - generalization

Generalization

1. Universal quantifiers

Generalizing allows the listener to go beyond his current thinking and open out to new ideas. A *universal quantifier* is a phrase that has a *universal* word in it, like 'all', 'everyone', everything' and also has no reference points that are specific to the experience of the listener, for example:

'And everything that you experience as you listen allows you to understand deeply...'

2. Modal operators

A modal operator is a word that implies possibility or necessity. A modal operator of possibility gives the listener permission, for example 'can' or 'may' or 'may not'.

'You may find you learn many new things...'

A modal operator of necessity allows the listener to form new rules of behaviour for himself, for example 'should', 'must'.

'You should take this opportunity to change...'

Milton Model - distortion

Distortion

1. Mind reading

In mind reading, you claim to know what is going on inside someone's head, for example: 'I know that you are understanding many new things about yourself as we are talking...'

2. Complex equivalence

Here you state one thing as being the equivalent of the other, for example: 'The fact that you are relaxing means that you are making sense of things.'

   In other words, *relaxing* becomes the *equivalent* of *making sense*. So as the person relaxes more, he accepts the suggestion that he will make more sense of things.

3. Nominalizations

A nominalization is a noun that 'can't be put into a box'. Because nominalizations are so vague, the person's unconscious mind has room to interpret them in a way that is appropriate for himself, for example: 'As your relaxation grows, you find new insights and excitements.'

4. Cause and effect

With cause and effect you imply that one thing is linked to another and causes it to happen. This allows you to take something you observe the other person experiencing and link it to an outcome you and he wants, for example: 'If you close your eyes, you will feel more relaxed.'

5. Presuppositions

A presupposition is an assumption that an outcome is going to happen, for example: 'I don't know how deep your trance is yet.'

   This presupposes you are in a trance and on hearing this the other person will in fact go into one.

Piecing it all together

To use the Milton Model with another person, you need to help him go into a light trance and then to use your language in such a way that his unconscious mind will have permission to start looking for resources that take it towards the outcome that you have set up with him.

The stages of the Milton Model

1. Pace current experience

First, pace the current experience of the person:

▶ Describe what the person is experiencing to him as he experiences it.

▶ Describe it in a way that is undeniable by him because what you are describing is what he is doing externally and involves no mind reading.

▶ This allows you and the other person to get into rapport and helps the person to go into trance.

> For example:
> 'You are sitting on the chair, listening to my voice [pacing] and as you are hearing it...you can begin to relax more [leading].'

2. Use general language

Talk in ambiguous, general and vague language. This allows you to talk to the person's unconscious mind and get his conscious mind out of the way. The ambiguity of the Milton Model language distracts and confuses the conscious mind, aiding the trance.

3. Use the Milton Model language patterns

Introduce the deletion, generalization and distortion language patterns of the Milton Model to allow the other person to begin to access his unconscious resources and start to change on an unconscious level.

You don't need to know what is happening. All you have to do while this is going on is to observe (calibrate) the other person's physiology so that you can see that pleasant changes are taking place.

4. Deepen the trance with additional language patterns

As well as the language patterns given above, there are several other ways of using the language that Milton used. These will all increase your effectiveness. We will look at these in more depth over the next few pages.

Putting it together: an example

'I know that you are understanding new things...and it's really great that you are understanding new things...because...that means...you're already learning more at an unconscious level than you think you understand...and it's good to let the unconscious learn in any way it wants to. And since you are sitting on the chair, listening to my words, all the things you are hearing are allowing you to have new insights. And you have, haven't you...?'

Additional Milton patterns

These are other language patterns that John Grinder and Richard Bandler modelled from Milton Erickson. You can use them to deepen a person's trance.

Double binds

A *double bind* is when you give someone a choice, but you set up the extent of the choice, for example: 'I don't know whether you might like to do it now or in a few minutes.' This is a simple double-bind statement. It appears to give the listener a choice, whereas in fact you have already predetermined how much choice that person will have as to when he will do it. In addition you have also presupposed that he will in fact do it.

Conversational postulates

A *conversational postulate* is a question that expects a 'yes' or a 'no' answer. It allows you to respond if you want to and so means that the person speaking does not sound authoritarian or directive to the person listening. Instead his language sounds permissive, as if the listener has choice. Nevertheless, the listener's unconscious mind understands the question as an instruction, for example: 'Do you feel this...is something you can imagine?' 'Can you consider for a moment...?'

Tag questions

A *tag question* is a question that is 'tagged on' to a statement, for example 'isn't it?', 'wouldn't you?', 'aren't they?' 'You can relax, can't you?' 'This is the quickest way to relax, isn't it?' A tag question softens the statement the questioner has made and therefore displaces resistance.

Tag questions that are ungrammatical, a mix of past and present tenses, can also be used to deliberately confuse the listener's conscious mind, for example: 'You can relax, didn't you?'

Embedded language

You can embed questions or commands by hiding them in a sentence. They are not heard by the conscious mind, but the unconscious mind hears them in the way that they are intended.

Mark the command or statement with a slight change in your voice, either by changing the volume or speed or by a slight pause after this portion of the statement. It is as if you have an auditory highlight pen around that portion of the sentence. For example: 'I don't know whether *you will go into trance right now.*' (Command). 'I don't know whether you know *what resources do you need to change now?*' (Question).

Extended quotes

Here you present a message to the listener in the form of a quotation from someone else. This is yet another way of sounding more permissive and less directive, as you distance yourself from any responsibility from what is being said. For example: 'I went to America once and met a man there who was very skilled at hypnosis and he used to say that he once met the greatest hypnotist ever who said that it was *the easiest thing in the world to go into a trance!*'

must know

Metaphors
Stories told to a purpose are known in NLP as *metaphors*. A story or metaphor is a great place to embed quotes, commands and questions. You can get a character in the story to say what you want the listener to hear and they will hear it uncritically.

Restriction violation

The unconscious loves listening to stories. When you tell a story you can give inanimate objects or animals feelings or powers that a human would have. This is known as *restriction violation*. For example: 'A fly can have feelings...' 'The chair has a secret to share with you...'

Ambiguity

Ambiguity as a language pattern is used to distract and confuse the conscious mind so that the speaker can access the listener's unconscious mind more quickly.

Types of ambiguity

Phonological ambiguity

'Hear/here', 'buy now/by now', 'you're unconscious/your unconscious' are words and phrases that sound alike but have different meanings. If you use ambiguous words like this in a statement, it will make the listener do a trans-derivational search.

Syntactic ambiguity

Syntactic ambiguity is where the syntactic function of a word is not clear from the context in which it is set. Generally this works by adding '-ing' to make a noun a verb. For example: 'They are interesting people.' *Are 'they' (whoever they are) interesting 'the people' or are the people themselves interesting?*

Scope ambiguity

Here you use a phrase where the context does not make it clear whether it applies to all or just one portion of the sentence. For example: 'The fascinating sounds and sights...' *Are the sights fascinating as well as the sounds?* 'Speaking to you as a woman...' *Am I a woman or are you?* 'The weight of your arms and legs...' *Are both your legs and arms heavy?*

Punctuation ambiguity

Here you let one sentence run into another. Again, this confuses the conscious mind. For example: 'I want you to notice your hand me the pen.'

must know

Link words

These words link sentences together smoothly, without interrupting the flow of thoughts the other person is having. They allow the listener to stay in his trance. They also imply that something will cause an effect. Powerful link words:

▶ and
▶ as
▶ while
▶ before
▶ when
▶ during
▶ since

7 Changing your viewpoint

Profound changes can sometimes come in your
life simply from changing your perceptions of a
situation in the past or present. NLP has several
techniques that you can use to look at life from
a new perspective. They will provide you with
more choice in your life and can enhance your
relationships with other people. One of the
central beliefs of NLP is that you hold all of
the resources you need inside you. Use these
resources to change your states of mind and
increase your motivation through the
techninque of *anchoring*.

Chunking

Chunking is an easy technique you can use to create new choices. When we deal with information, we break it up or 'chunk' it in order to make it easier to deal with. Sometimes we use large or 'big picture' chunks. Sometimes we use small or 'detail' chunks.

must know

To chunk up on a habit or behaviour, ask 'What is the positive intention behind this behaviour?'
To chunk upon your outcomes, ask, 'If I have this outcome what will that give me?'

Levels of chunking

People can habitually think at either a big picture, general, large chunk level, or at a detailed, specific, small chunk level. Miscommunication can arise if one person is focusing at a different level from another.

To create communication, you can 'chunk up' or 'down' or 'sideways' to meet the other person at a level that he can understand. This is a very effective technique to use in negotiation to get a win-win scenario. When you chunk differently it gives you a new perspective on an issue.

How to chunk up, down and sideways

To move from the specific to the general, ask, 'What is this an example of?'

To move from the general to the specific, ask, 'What is an example of this?'

For example: Person A and B are negotiating over what to eat.

Person A says, 'I want to eat pizza.'

Person B says, 'I want to eat pasta.'

What are both these foods examples of? Italian

food. Therefore the two people can agree to go to an Italian restaurant.

To move sideways, ask, 'What is another example of this?'

The Meta Model chunks from general to specific. The Milton Model chunks from specific to general. *(See also Chapter 11.)*

The model of chunking *(see below)* is known as the Hierarchy of Ideas.

FROM BIG PICTURE TO DETAIL

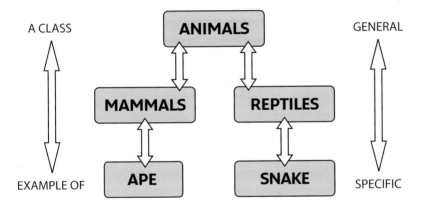

CHUNKING SIDEWAYS

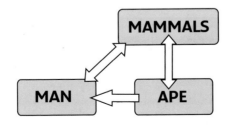

Perceptual positions

We naturally take different positions at different times. Sometimes we see things very strongly only from our own vantage point. At other times, we step into other people's shoes and look at the world from that perspective. Sometimes we may stand back from a situation totally so that we can look dispassionately at what is happening.

Different viewpoints

These different viewpoints are called *perceptual positions* in NLP. They were developed by John Grinder and Judith DeLozier into the *perceptual positions technique*, drawing on work originally done by Gregory Bateson. The technique allows you to gain multiple perspectives on a particular interaction.

It is important to realize that there is no such thing as one 'correct' perspective. Each person has only a partial understanding and sees things through his own blinkers. You don't have to agree with the views of another person, but if you can see things from that person's perspective it stops you being rigid in your thinking and opens up greater levels of understanding.

When to use the perceptual positions technique

You can use this technique either to look at a situation after it has happened (review), or before it has happened (mental rehearsal/preview). It is particularly useful where there is a block in understanding between the people involved or where you feel stuck in a particular way of thinking about a situation.

It can be used in business negotiations. Any resolution of a relationship conflict or a negotiation involves the perspectives of all the people involved and coming up with a solution that allows everyone to feel satisfied – a 'win-win' scenario.

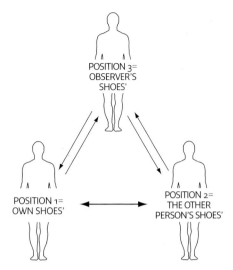

POSITION 3= OBSERVER'S SHOES'

POSITION 1= OWN SHOES'

POSITION 2= THE OTHER PERSON'S SHOES'

The three positions of the technique:
1. **Position one/first perspective: you**
2. **Position two/second perspective: the other person**
3. **Position three/third perspective: an observer**

Perceptual positions technique
This is a useful technique because:
▶ It throws light on what other people may be thinking and you can gain new insights into their viewpoints.
▶ It gives you more flexibility by opening out your thinking.
▶ You can stand back and gain some objectivity about an issue.
▶ You will have new choices through understanding how the dynamics of the situation have worked.
▶ You can see the effects your own behaviour and communication have on others.
▶ Everyone involved can reach a win-win solution to a negotiation or deal.

The technique

1. In your mind, put yourself into each of the positions in turn.
2. In position one, see the situation through your own eyes, as if it is happening to you. Notice your own opinions, your views about events and your values. What does it look like, sound like and feel like to you from your own perspective? What do you feel emotionally? What are you thinking? What are your beliefs and outcomes?
3. In position two, put yourself in the other person's shoes. How is that person thinking about the same situation? Imagine what he feels to be true about the situation he is in. What does it look like, sound like and feel like from his perspective? What are his beliefs and outcomes?
4. In the third position, what do you observe about the relationship between the people in positions one and two? What new perspective do you get here? What do the two positions have in common? How are they related? Pay attention to their communication and their non-verbal behaviour. What are the common elements in their outcomes? What advice can you give them from your objective position?
5. Now repeat the process again.
6. At the end of the round, step back into your own shoes in position one. Notice what you have learned about yourself, the other person and the whole situation. What new choices do you have available to you now?

The Meta Mirror

The Meta Mirror is a further technique, developed by Robert Dilts, that draws on the ideas of perceptual positions. In this technique, you use different positions to look at another person's viewpoint. It adds a fourth position to the three in the previous technique.

When to use this technique

You can either do the technique inside your head or actually move around to each position in turn. In this technique, the idea is that how another person treats you is a reflection of the way you see and behave towards yourself.

You can use this technique to review or preview a meeting where you will be talking to another person about an issue you don't entirely agree on, or after an interaction in which you didn't come to a positive conclusion for both of you. If you have something to say to another person and you don't know what their reaction will be, do this technique and imagine how that person will respond to what you have to say to him.

How to do the technique

Decide what interaction/relationship you would like to use this technique for. It might be an unsatisfactory conversation you had with another person. If this is the first time you have used the technique, choose a situation where it will be helpful to improve communication but not the worst relationship you have.

must know

The Meta Mirror is a 'content-free' technique. You do not need to discuss the content of the situation you are recalling or previewing. It works best by you processing your thoughts inside yourself.

1. In position one (self), look at the other person and ask yourself, 'What do I see, hear, feel and think in this position about the relationship/interaction?'
2. Then step into the other person's shoes, position two. Imagine how the situation looks from that person's point of view. If it helps, get into his way of sitting or standing.

3. Now, go to position three. Be an observer, detached from the situation. Notice the relationship between the two people (one and two). What do you notice about their relationship and their interaction?

4. Add another position (position four) from which you can observe the interaction between the two people as well as the observer (positions one to three). Notice the relationship between position one and position three and the insights position three has had about position one. Notice the same for positions two and three.

5. Finally, go back to each position in turn, thinking about any additional resources and insights you have when you take this perspective and would like to integrate for the future as a conscious resource. End by coming back to yourself in the now. Think of a time in the future when these resources and insights you have discovered in yourself may be useful. Notice how you will know that it is time to access these new resources you have just gained from this exercise.

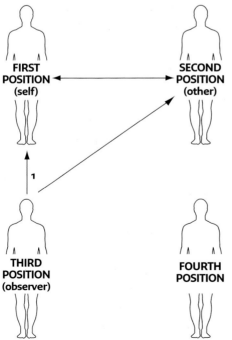

FIRST POSITION (self)

SECOND POSITION (other)

1

THIRD POSITION (observer)

FOURTH POSITION

must know

The Meta Mirror is a safe context in which you can shift positions to deal with limitations, conflicts and issues inside the dynamic of the relationship to produce an outcome that is positive for all the parties involved.

Reframing

Have you ever changed the frame on a picture? How did it look to you with a smaller frame or a bigger frame?

Putting a frame around your thinking

Imagine that it is raining outside in the middle of summer. Is that a good thing or a bad thing? If you are a farmer or a gardener, you will be very happy to get some water for your plants. However if you have arranged a picnic for a family outing, you won't be happy at all.

Negative emotions about an event or situation are not caused by the event itself but by how you see it and respond to it. However by looking at things from a different perspective, you can create positive emotions and new choices.

Changing the frame

By changing how you look at something – the angle or perspective from which you view it – you can change your whole viewpoint about the meaning of what you are looking at. Nothing has meaning *in and of itself*. We give it meaning.

You can *reframe* what you choose to see by making one aspect of a situation more significant than another. The frame you put around it will determine what you pay attention to. Reframing is the means by which you can choose what reaction you will have to any given situation. It will liberate you from negativity and stop you feeling that you are a victim of events.

How to change your view

If you change the

▶ situation
▶ time frame

your perceptions of the same situation will change, because all meaning is dependent upon the context in which it is set. Jokes, fairy tales and children's stories are full of reframes. In some fairy tales, a situation might arise that the reader views as terrible, however, by the end of the story you realize that all was not as it seemed. For example, in the story *The Ugly Duckling*, the ugliest duckling turns out to be a beautiful swan.

What if you were to lose your job? In the short term, it might seem like a disaster for many reasons. But if you look at it in a longer time frame, you might realize that it gives you the chance to take a step back and to reassess what it is you want out of life. Perhaps you could go on to start a completely new career in a different area entirely.

Words as frames

The words and phrases we use can be used as frames to point to the particular meaning we want others to hear:

▶ 'Unfortunately...he lost his job.'
▶ 'Amazingly...he lost his job.'
▶ 'The exchange rate is up – that's good news for importers.'
▶ 'The exchange rate is up – that's good news for exporters.'
▶ 'The price is £1,999. That's under £2,000.'
▶ 'The price is £1,999. That's nearly £2,000.'

Context reframes and meaning reframes

You can break reframes down into two types: context and meaning. Both reframes ask you to look at how a behaviour could have a different value or meaning if you look at it in a different way.

Context reframes

Here are a few responses that signal you are using a context reframe: 'I'm too...' 'He's too...' 'I wish I could do this more...' When a person uses these words, he is complaining that he (or another person) acts in a particular way in a particular context. That person has generalized the behaviour and deleted the fact that this behaviour takes place within a specific context.

How to context reframe

You can respond to this kind of statement by pointing out that the same behaviour may be useful in a different context, for example:

▶ 'He's too...detail-orientated for this job.'
▶ 'She's too easy-going to tell her staff off when they do something wrong.'

Think of a different context in which the person will respond differently to the same behaviour, for example:

▶ 'He would be a great proofreader – it needs a lot of attention to detail.'
▶ 'She's easy-going. She always has lots of friends as a result.'

must know

A basic belief in NLP is that you behave in the way you behave for a reason and that reason is positive.

Meaning reframe

You can use a meaning (i.e. content) reframe when you do not like your own response to particular events to form a more positive response.

How to meaning reframe

Ask yourself, 'What else could this behaviour mean? What is the positive value of this behaviour?' Or, if you are doing this with another person, ask yourself: 'What is it that this person hasn't noticed (in this context) that will bring about a different meaning and change his response?'

For example: 'When I have to do public speaking, I start to feel anxious.' What is the positive value of this behaviour? Perhaps it is that you make yourself prepare thoroughly. It gives you motivation and adrenaline that will help you to give a better speech.

Applying reframing to your own life

See if you can come up with examples from your own life of events you would like to see in a more positive light. Think of something you have classified as a 'mistake'. Apply a context reframe and a meaning reframe. How could either of these techniques allow you to develop a different view about what you experienced?

What does reframing do to the meaning of the experience? Notice if you begin to highlight or focus on different aspects of the experience. What are the advantages of the situation that you can now make work for you? For example, you may have chosen to take a job with a firm, but you have ethical concerns about a product that the company produces so you resign. However you did learn some skills at the job, and you can bring these to a job that you find more rewarding.

Six-step reframe

What if you want to stop a habit but you keep on doing it?

Changing unconscious behaviour

The six-step reframe technique addresses behaviour that you cannot change consciously. If you have changed the way you behave but then start behaving that way again, it may be that you are getting what is known as *secondary gain* from that behaviour. In other words, it is giving you a benefit that you are not conscious of as well as the ones you realize you are getting from it.

With this technique you don't need to know the intention consciously. You can use it for:

▶ Changing unwanted behaviour that persists and/or is habitual
▶ Addressing secondary gain
▶ Dealing with mental/emotional blocks
▶ Dealing with behaviour that seems to stop and then surfaces again
▶ A physical symptom

How to six-step reframe

You can do this with yourself or with another person.

1. Identify the unwanted behaviour or feeling (the problem)

This could be, for example, smoking, overeating, nail-biting, a physical symptom with no obvious cause. Obviously for any symptom you are worried about, always check with your doctor first.

2. Establish communication with the part of the unconscious mind that is responsible for this behaviour

▶ Go inside your head and ask if you can establish contact with the part of you that is responsible for this behaviour or for resisting the behaviour you desire. Remember that the part has a positive intention, so address it in a friendly way. Even if the behaviour is harmful to you, the intention of the responsible part is positive.

▶ Ask this part to give you a signal. Ask yourself: 'Is the unconscious mind willing to communicate consciously?'

▶ You may receive words inside your head or a physical signal such as the movement of a finger in response.

▶ Thank the part and ask it to increase the response to signify a 'yes'. You should get the same signal again.

3. Discover the positive intention of the part that drives the unwanted behaviour or feeling and separate it from the unwanted behaviour

▶ Ask the part what its intention is for you. First ask if it is willing to reveal its intention: 'Is the unconscious mind willing to communicate its intention?'

▶ If you get a 'yes' signal, say: 'Have it communicate its intention.'

▶ Pay attention to whatever words come into your mind. This is the most crucial step in reframing.

▶ If the words you get are negatively expressed, for example 'I don't want to be hurt', ask what the *positive intention* of these words is. Eventually you will get the intention expressed in a positive way, for example 'I want to be happy.'

▶ Thank the part for revealing its intention.

▶ If you do not get a clear answer, assume that you are getting the answers on an unconscious level and continue to the next step.

4. Generate alternative behaviour that satisfies the intention

▶ Once you know the intention of the behaviour, ask the creative part of yourself if it would be willing to achieve the same positive intention in other ways. (We all have a creative part, as your unconscious mind is infinitely resourceful.)

▶ Ask it to come up with at least three alternative ways to achieve the same intention. You could say: ' There have been times when I've been creative, whether I knew it or not. Now can the unconscious mind search through all my memories and generate at least three alternatives that will completely satisfy [name the positive intention]?'

▶ You may get the answers consciously, however you do not need to know them consciously. Trust that your creative part will come up with the right answers.

5. Future pace

▶ Get agreement from your unconscious that it will use one of these new choices of behaviour. Check for a 'yes' signal by asking: 'Is the unconscious mind willing to take responsibility for implementing these alternatives?'

▶ If it is not willing, repeat step 4 and ask for some additional choices.

6. Check it is good for you

▶ Mentally rehearse the new behaviour in your mind in different times and locations. The point is to make sure there is no other block or resistance.

▶ Ask: 'Does the unconscious mind need to make any other adjustments to ensure the success of this change? Are all parts of me in agreement on these new choices? Do any parts object to these new choices?'

▶ If you meet any resistance, go back to step 4 and generate some alternative choices that will meet the intention of any other parts that have surfaced.

▶ Then go through steps 5 and 6 again until all resistance is dealt with.

Anchors

Anchors are a very simple way to tap into your unconscious resources. An anchor is an unconscious trigger that can be applied to produce a positive state of mind and to change your behaviour.

Anchors can be set up deliberately to give you choice and emotional freedom so that you can function at your best in any situation, especially those where in the past you have felt negative or unresourceful. The technique is based on the core belief of NLP that we already have all the resources inside ourselves to be and get whatever we want. It is just a case of getting hold of the resources when we want them.

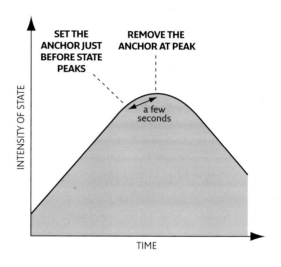

Anchors work by creating an association between an emotion and an external trigger. This response can be 'conditioned' or made automatic.

Everyday anchors

Anchors occur in everyday life. They are set up automatically by an intense emotion that has become linked to an experience. When you come into contact with the anchor at a later date it triggers off some of the original associations. If the emotion, has been very intense it may set up a *phobia*. If it is less intense but the experience has occurred again and again, it may still set up an anchor subsequently.

Behavioural psychologists would point out that our behaviour is composed of anchors There are many naturally occurring anchors in everyday life that change our mood from one moment to another.

Negative and positive states

In everyday life, the states that are produced by naturally occurring anchors can be either positive or negative. A certain way of speaking, a particular facial expression and/or gesture can trigger off anger, or leave you feeling depressed or sad, and these feelings often occur to a greater extent than seems logical in the context. Why? Because a past experience has anchored you to a negative emotion linked to these experiences. For example if when you were a baby, your parents always managed to calm you down after a tantrum by speaking to you in a particular tone, it may well work later in life too.

Pavlov

The Soviet scientist Ivan Pavlov famously experimented on dogs to show how conditioning can trigger a response. When he sounded a tuning fork at the same time as feeding a dog a steak, the idea of the steak and the sound became linked together neurologically in the dog's brain. When he took the steak away and still sounded the tuning fork, the dog still salivated. Out of this came the idea that you can apply a specific stimulus to any intense experience and link the two together.

Anchors and the senses

Random everyday anchors can occur in all five senses: visual, auditory, kinaesthetic, gustatory (taste) and olfactory (smell).

Sensory anchors

If you *smell* a scent that you link with someone you are or were in love with, you will feel some emotion because the smell has triggered an association with the past feeling. How a piece of satin *feels* might bring back the memory of a wedding dress.

Consider what you feel when you *hear* the sound of a fire engine or police siren. This may depend on whether you have had any negative experiences with fire or the police. What about the *sight* of a school desk like the ones you used when a child? The *taste* of a food you have only had on a sunny and happy holiday might bring back some of the happiness you felt then even if you are eating it on a cold and miserable day at work.

Some anchors can occur in more than one representational system. The sight and sound of a police siren flashing red would be an example of an auditory and visual anchor. The taste and smell of fresh coffee might work as an anchor. The taste, sight and feel of a cigarette might also all be anchors.

Everyday triggers

Auditory
▶ telephone bell
▶ motorcycle motor
▶ train whistle

Visual
▶ a smile
▶ a frown
▶ a fist gesture

Olfactory/gustatory (smell and/or taste)
▶ fresh bread
▶ bacon and eggs frying
▶ cigarette smoke

Kinaesthetic (touch and feel)
▶ a hand on your back
▶ freshly washed sheets on your bed
▶ a sheepskin rug under your feet

Resource anchors

A resource anchor is a specific anchor that you deliberately set in order to change your emotional state and to bring positive resources into a situation.

How to set resource anchors

It may be useful to set up different resource anchors for different situations. Here are a few possible positive and resourceful states you might want to consider: happy, joyful, confident, highly motivated, completely relaxed, loving, elated. On the following pages are the steps to setting up a resource anchor.

1. Decide on a positive state

First of all, decide what state would be most positive for you in a particular context. If you are stressed, what would be a good alternative? How about if you are about to go into a meeting you are a little nervous about? What would be a good emotion to be feeling as you walk through the door? Choose a strong experience and a compelling state.

2. Elicit and calibrate the state

Think of the state(s) that you want to anchor. Elicit that state by going back to a memory of a time when you naturally felt that way. Make sure you are *associated* into the past experience – you are experiencing it as if you are there now. (A dissociated memory won't evoke the same emotion.) If you are not finding it easy to get into the state straightaway, shift your body around.

Working with others

If you are working with another person, model the state you want that person to get into – i.e. adjust your body and get into the state yourself. Then ask him questions to guide them into the state.

> **must know**
>
> **How to set a resource anchor**
> 1. Decide on a positive state.
> 2. Elicit and calibrate the state.
> 3. Select an anchor: visual, auditory or kinaesthetic.
> 4. Anchor the state.
> 5. Test the anchor to make sure it works.
> 6. 'Future pace' the anchor.

If you have good rapport with the person, you can *lead* him into the state (see pages 70–71). We are very influenced by what state other people are in when we produce particular states in ourselves. If everyone around you is feeling happy and elated, you will follow suit if you are in rapport with them.

Elicit the state

Tell yourself/the other person:
'Think of a *specific* time in the past when you felt this positive state. Go back to this time. See what you saw. Feel what you felt. Hear what you heard.'

As you are doing this you are associating into the experience and you will find that you are experiencing the emotion as if it is happening to you right now. If you now apply a stimulus/anchor at the peak of the experience, next time you want to get the feeling back all you have to do is to reapply the anchor and you will feel the same way.

Calibrate the state

Remember, 'to calibrate' means 'to observe what changes are happening in another person using your powers of observation'. If you are helping another person to get into a resourceful state, you will need to calibrate that person to make sure that he really is feeling the appropriate amount of emotion.

3. Select an anchor

Choose an anchor – it can be a visual, auditory or kinaesthetic one. For example, if you were using a kinaesthetic anchor, a good one would be to touch your knuckle because it is not a place that people normally touch. Another effective anchor would be to touch your heart, as this too is likely to be a unique anchor.

4. Anchor the state

As the experience/state approaches its peak of intensity, anchor it by touching your knuckle with your finger. As soon as the experience peaks, let go. This is to avoid anchoring a second state. You will need to hold your finger down for a period of between 5 and 15 seconds, no more.

Stacking states

If you want to experience more than one state, you can anchor more than one state at the same time. Break state (see page 49) by thinking about something else for a few seconds. If you are anchoring someone else, ask him an unrelated question. This will take his mind out of the previous state.

Anchor the next state in the same place in the same way. Break state and then continue stacking several states in this manner. You can add to this anchor any time that you are in a positive state so that it will become more and more powerful for you every time you use it.

> **must know**
>
> *Firing an anchor* means setting it off. With a kinaesthetic anchor you would touch the anchor for a few seconds to trigger off the feelings in your body. With a visual anchor you would look at it. With an auditory anchor you would listen to it.

5. Test the anchor

Test the anchor to see whether it works. Fire the anchor by touching the same place on your knuckle with your finger. What happens? If you have anchored the state(s) correctly you will observe a shift in yourself (or the other person if you are working with someone else). How do you feel now? Do you feel it is as compelling as you want it to be? What can you see, hear and feel? Is it different from before? If not, go back and stack some more states (or the same state again).

6. Future pace

Think of a situation some time in the future where in the past you might have felt unresourceful or negative. (Or take the other person through this process.) Imagine firing off the anchor. How positive do you feel at this point in the future?

> **must know**
>
> **Four keys to successful resource anchors**
> ▶ Anchor an intense feeling/state
> ▶ Anchor the feeling/state at the peak of its intensity
> ▶ Choose a unique anchor
> ▶ Make your anchor something that is easy to replicate

Collapse anchors

Collapse anchors can be used to get rid of negative states and to set up new choices. If you anchor two states then trigger them at the same time, the weaker one collapses into the stronger one.

watch out!

If you are collapsing anchors with another person, make sure you have a good rapport with him or the technique may not work effectively as you will not get into the same states.

Collapse the negative

To get rid of a negative feeling stack a series of strong, compelling positive states in the same way that you would for a resource anchor and collapse the negative state into it. The next time you try to access the negative state it will bring up the positive state because the two will be linked together neurologically. This leaves a feeling of a neutral emotion.

How to collapse anchors

1. Choose the negative or unresourceful state you are going to collapse.
2. Choose appropriate positive states to stack. You can either stack one state as a resource anchor several times or choose several different positive states.
3. Anchor the positive states you have chosen onto one of your/the person's knuckles in the same way as for a resource anchor. Repeat this several times. If you are working with another person, make sure he is associated into the state. Help him by getting into the state too.
4. Break state. If you are working with another person, ask him to do something to focus his attention elsewhere for a few minutes. This takes you out of the positive states.
5. Elicit and calibrate the negative state. Anchor the negative state *once* only on a *different* knuckle.
6. *Fire* the two anchors together by touching the knuckles at the same time. Watch as the states come up to peak and integration takes place.
7. If working with another person, calibrate to check that integration has taken place. You will notice changes in his skin colour, breathing and other physical changes within a few seconds.
8. As soon as integration has occurred, release your finger from the negative anchor first while continuing to hold down the positive anchor for a further 5 seconds.
9. Break state. When you are working with someone else, ask him to do something to focus his attention elsewhere for a few minutes.
10. Test the anchor. Fire the negative anchor by touching your knuckle or asking the other person to touch his knuckle. If it works, you will feel/notice a neutral rather than a negative state.

Chaining anchors

Naturally occurring states can work in chains. One anchor triggers off a state, that then triggers off another state, potentially spiralling into a more negative feeling over a period of time. You can design a chain of anchors to replace this and to take you from an unresourceful state to a more positive state.

How to chain anchors

1. Identify the state you no longer want to feel. If you are working with another person, make sure you have named it in specific terms using that person's language.
2. Choose the positive and resourceful state you would like to feel instead. Again, if you are working with another person, make sure you have named it in specific terms using his language.
3. What states would best take you from the beginning state to the end state? Choose at least one link state.
4. Elicit and calibrate the first state. Anchor it to knuckle number one.
5. Break state and test it to make sure it is anchored correctly.
6. Anchor the next states to different knuckles. Break state between each one and test them.
7. Fire anchor one. As you reach the peak of the state, hold down anchor one and fire anchor two (state 2). If you are working with another person, ask him to signal you when he is reaching the peak of the state, then hold down anchor one and fire anchor two.
8. Release anchor one and hold anchor two. As anchor two reaches the peak of the state, fire anchor three (state 3) while holding anchor two.
9. Repeat this process until you reach the final anchor. Let go of the final anchor. Break state.
10. Repeat the whole chain in the same way three times.
11. Fire anchor one. It should move you/the person through the whole chain of states so that you/he go into the end state automatically.
12. Future pace the chain. Imagine (or ask the person to imagine) a time in the future where in the past you (he) would have felt the old unresourceful state. Do you go into the positive state instead? Calibrate to check that the person goes into a positive state.

must know

Linking states
It is best not to have more than three states as links. Make these states pleasant. For example, first state: nervousness; link state: calmness; end state: confidence. Check that the chain has appropriate and resourceful states.

8 Removing blocks

You may have internal resistance or blocks
to overcome on the way to achieving your
outcomes. Limitations are nothing more than
habitual ways of thinking that have led you
to block off avenues for action, changes in
your behaviour or possibilities for different
outcomes. They are simply rules you have
set up for the way you currently play the game
of life. This chapter outlines a number of
techniques you can use to change the rules
of this game.

Aligned and congruent change

Before you begin to make changes to your life, find out how congruently you want your outcome. Taking action is one of the best means you have to extract deeply held beliefs, emotions, conflicts and decisions that might block or limit you in some way from achieving a particular outcome.

watch out!

Underlying every behaviour is a positive intention. Therefore, always make sure you take account of all the benefits you get from your current situation and find other ways to satisfy them when you make changes to your life.

Congruence

If you are not congruent about your changes, as you start to take action your unconscious may throw up *doubts* or *reasons* why you can't carry on towards it. As soon as you come up against a block to your outcome, you can use one of the many techniques that NLP has to remove the block.

Chunking

We have already discussed how chunking at a different level can shed new light on a situation (see pages 118–19). When you are faced with a block, you can use chunking to understand why it is there and how you can become more congruent about getting your outcome.

Chunking up

You can do this by *chunking up*. If you are having problems changing a way of behaving, ask yourself: 'What does this behaviour do for me?' or 'What is the purpose of this?' If you are having problems moving towards an outcome, ask yourself: 'What will this outcome do for me?'

Chunking down

You can also *chunk down*. With an outcome, ask yourself: 'What prevents me from achieving this outcome?' With behaviour, ask yourself, 'What other way/of behaving would satisfy the same outcome?'

The Logical Levels Model

It is important that when you remove blocks you not only meet your unconscious needs but also create a change that lasts. One way to do this is to make sure that the changes you make are aligned at all levels of your being. A useful model to refer to is the Logical Levels or Neurological Levels Model.

Change at different levels

This model was developed by the American NLP writer and trainer Robert Dilts and inspired by the work of Gregory Bateson. According to this model, the process of learning and change takes place at the different levels inside the mind.

There are six basic levels to the model, structured as a hierarchy. The more abstract (or higher) levels dominate the less abstract (lower) levels. A change at a lower level may have a slight influence or no influence on a higher level. But a change at a higher level inevitably influences the lower levels. The levels are as follows:

1. Environment: where and when

'I find I can't achieve anything in this *environment*. It all goes wrong when I am *here*.'

At the bottom of the model is the first level – your environment. Where and when something occurs can influence your success in a given situation, your ability to build rapport with others or the amount of change you produce. In other words, context – or 'being in the right place at the right time' – can have a great influence on your results. One location may offer you great opportunities while another may constrain your abilities. You might find that moving cities, countries, offices or home can produce increased or reduced work opportunities or better friendships.

2. Behaviour: what

'I don't want to do *that*.'

The second level in the Logical Levels Model is behaviour. This is what someone does. Every action we take is a proactive move towards or a reaction to a purpose. The purpose is either an outcome we have decided on or something that we are entirely unconscious of. Unwanted behaviour such as overeating or nail-biting may have to be tackled at several neurological levels before it can be overcomed.

3. Capability/skills: how

'I wish I found it easy to *take action*. I don't know how to.'

The third level is how you do things – the everyday skills you use as well as the strategies you follow. At this level, the skills are used unconsciously so they constitute what we consider habits. Some of these skills were consciously acquired, for example learning to drive. Others are learned automatically or with minimum thought early in life such as speaking our native language.

4. Beliefs and values: why

'The world doesn't work like that.'

Beliefs are our enabling or disabling thoughts – what we think of as a 'fact' or the 'truth'. Values are what are important to us. If you believe you are too ugly to ever have a relationship, when you meet someone who is interested in you, you may find it difficult to believe that the person really cares for you. You may even question what is wrong with that person if he could be interested in you. If you believe you are a very likeable person and value friendships, you will probably find yourself surrounded by friends.

5. Identity: who

'*I* am a bad person.'

Identity is who you believe you are – your sense of self. It is made up of your core beliefs and values as well as your purpose and mission in life. Because an identity is supported very strongly by many different beliefs, change that occurs at this level will generally be more comprehensive than changing a single belief, value or skill.

6. Spirituality: purpose

'I have lost any sense of a higher *purpose*.'

Your sense of connection with something above or beyond is the highest level. This is the level of a general spirituality or religion. Here the questions you might ask yourself are: 'What is my purpose here on Earth?' 'Why am I here?' For an organization the questions would be similar and focused on purpose or ethics: 'Why are we here?' 'How can we contribute to the greater world?'

Any change at this neurological level can have an immediate influence on all the other levels. We have all heard of people who have had spiritual conversions that led them to give up well-paid jobs for something more fulfilling such as charity work in a foreign country. This type of spirital change can mean giving up families, possessions and even lives.

How the Logical Levels model works

Successful outcomes and individuals are aligned throughout all six levels. Here is an example:

- ▶ *Spirituality:* 'My purpose is to bring good to the world.'
- ▶ *Identity:* 'I am a good person.'
- ▶ *Beliefs and values:* 'Social work helps needy people and is a good thing.'
- ▶ *Capability:* 'I have the skills and talents to help the people who are needy.'
- ▶ *Behaviour:* 'Every day I meet people and help them.'
- ▶ *Environment:* 'The place I live and work in has lots of people who need help.'

LOGICAL LEVELS MODEL

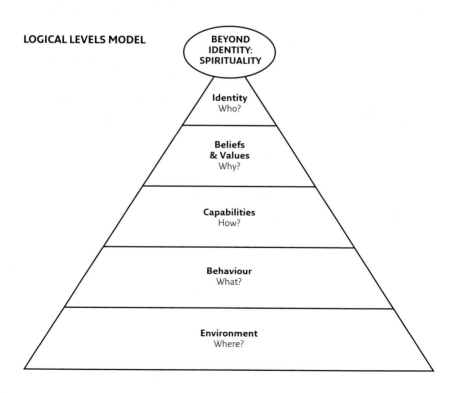

BEYOND IDENTITY: SPIRITUALITY

Identity
Who?

Beliefs & Values
Why?

Capabilities
How?

Behaviour
What?

Environment
Where?

Changing beliefs that limit you

Do you have any beliefs about yourself or the world that stop you achieving your outcomes or make you feel negative about yourself?

What do you really believe?

Be accurate about what you *really* believe rather than what you feel you 'should' believe. As soon as you identify the beliefs you don't want, you can change them.

Identifying beliefs

The easiest way to identify your beliefs is to do a simple brainstorm with yourself. Take each main area of your life in turn and ask yourself: 'What do I believe about [this area of my life]?' Answer: 'I believe...' 'I do not believe...'

List anything that comes into your mind, however illogical or irrational it sounds to you right now. Go on writing until you run out of anything to write. Examine what you have written.

❏ Are these useful beliefs for you to hold?

❏ Do any of these beliefs limit you, either generally in getting the maximum out of life or in this context in particular?

❏ What belief might be more useful for you to hold?

Modelling successful beliefs

What would be useful beliefs for you to hold? You may be able to think of some straightaway. You may be able to think of a successful person you could model:

▶ Who do you know personally who has useful and positive beliefs in the area in which you want to change your beliefs?

▶ In what way do that person's beliefs differ from the beliefs you hold?

▶ What does he believe about himself?

▶ What does he believe about the world?

▶ What does he believe about the subject you are thinking about?

Submodalities

We all make our own experience of the world. *Submodalities* are the way in which we store or code our experience inside our brains. They consist of using internal visual images, sounds and feelings.

Submodalities
The world is represented inside your brain through *submodalities*. These are principally visual, auditory and kinaesthetic, but also olfactory and gustatory.

Submodalities

Visual submodality questions
- ❏ Is it bright or dim?
- ❏ Focused or unfocused?
- ❏ Colour or black and white?
- ❏ Where is it located?
- ❏ Is it big or small?
- ❏ Framed or panoramic?
- ❏ Movie or still?
- ❏ Are you dissociated, seeing yourself in the picture?
- ❏ Or is it as if you are seeing the picture through your own eyes, associated?

Kinesthetic submodality questions
- ❏ Where can you feel this?
- ❏ Is there a temperature or weight, size or shape?
- ❏ How about movement and duration?
- ❏ Is there a texture?

Auditory submodality questions
- ❏ Is the sound loud or soft, fast or slow?
- ❏ Does it have a rhythm?
- ❏ Is it continuous or broken up?

Checking submodalities

Think for a moment of a time when you felt really happy. Notice if you have a picture. Notice the visual distinctions within the picture. These are the *visual submodalities*.

Do you have any feelings in your body when you think of this time? Is there a kinaesthetic element to the representation you have in your mind? What about any auditory elements?

What can you hear? Is there a sound associated with this image? Now think of a time when you were feeling a different emotion. What is your picture this time? How about any auditory or kinaesthetic elements?

As you do this you will notice that every state and emotion is encoded differently within our brains. There may be two or three key submodality differences between the two representations, the happy memory and your other memory.

must know

Critical submodalities
The visual submodalities that often make a 'critical' difference are usually brightness, the focus of the picture, whether you are associated or dissociated and the distance you are away from the picture.

How to change beliefs using submodalities

We hold our beliefs inside our brains in the same way as our emotions, using pictures or auditory and kinaesthetic submodalities. You can change your beliefs by simply changing the picture of that belief that you store inside your brain. By changing the encoding of the belief, for example by changing the submodalities to those of a different belief, the first belief will actually become the second belief.

You can use this technique for getting rid of limiting and disempowering beliefs.

1. Identify a belief you hold to be true.

2. Identify a belief you don't hold to be true (*non-belief*).

3. Check the submodalities of each one (*see table opposite*). As you think of each belief, what are the submodalities of that belief – the pictures, sounds and feelings that make it up? You should only pay attention to these features that *structure* the picture, not the *content* of the picture.

4. To find out the critical submodalities (*drivers*), compare the two lists you have for each belief. What are the differences?

5. If you switch the submodalities of the picture you have for your belief into the one you have for your non-belief, you will find that you no longer hold the original belief.

Advanced belief change: installing a new belief

You can use this technique for yourself or another person. Use the way you store a belief (submodalities) to put a positive, answering belief in place of an old belief that no longer helps you.

must know

When you are working with other people, you will probably be able to install new beliefs using visual submodalities.

watch out!

To change beliefs, use the belief change script *(see previous pages)*. But to change habits or behaviour, use a swish pattern.

Installing a new belief

Part one

▶ Think of a belief about yourself that you wish you did not have (belief one).

▶ As you think of that belief, what are the submodalities – the pictures, sounds and feelings that make it up? Only pay attention to the features that structure the picture. Do not think about the content of the picture.

▶ Next, think of a belief that you used to have but that is no longer true (belief two). For example, you used to be a child, so in the past you also used to *believe* you were a child. Now that you have grown up that belief it is no longer true.

▶ When you think of that past belief, what picture do you have in your mind? What are the submodalities – the pictures, sounds and feelings that make it up?

▶ Now compare the list of submodalities you have for beliefs one and two. You will find that there are some key differences. For example, one may be in black and white and one in colour, or the size or location may be different. Maybe one has auditory or kinaesthetic submodalities and the other has none. These differences show the ways in which you store different types of belief in your brain.

▶ Get the picture back in your mind for belief one. Now use your list of submodalities for belief two. Change the picture you have into the submodalities of belief two. For example if belief one was associated, and belief two was dissociated, make the picture dissociated.

▶ Test your original belief. You should find that you no longer believe it, as you have converted it into a belief that used to be true but is no longer true by coding it in a different way in your brain.

Part two

▶ Now think of a belief that is absolutely true for you (belief three). Think of something so definite there is absolutely no doubt attached to it at all, for example the belief that you live on this planet.

▶ Check whether you have a picture and then check the submodalities – all the visual, auditory and kinaesthetic qualities. There may be submodalities in each category or only in one category. It doesn't matter. Again, ignore the content of the picture and focus on the qualities of the picture.

▶ Think of a belief that you don't yet believe but you would like to have (belief four). This is probably the opposite of belief one that limited you. What are its submodalities?

▶ Now compare the list of submodalities you have for beliefs three and four. You will find again that there are some key differences because of the way you code your different beliefs in your brain.

▶ Change the submodalities of the belief that you want to be true into the submodalities of the belief that is absolutely true.

▶ Now test your new beliefs. What do you believe? You will find that you have a new belief that is absolutely true for you.

must know

Make the present-state picture associated because this 'fixes it' in the past in your brain. Make the desired state disassociated. This sets it up in your brain as a direction in which to move.

Swish pattern

A visual *swish pattern* is used to change behaviour through changing the way you code that behaviour in your brain.

Swish pattern technique

1. First identify the behaviour or habit you want to change (present state). It may be something you do, for example eat too much chocolate, or something you don't do, for example act confidently in a certain situation.
2. Get a picture of the behaviour. How do you know when to do it? What is the visual trigger for it? Is it a picture inside your head? Or something you see in the real world?
3. Make the picture associated.
4. Identify the critical submodalities that make the picture what it is. Size, location and brightness are often critical submodalities. Now play with them to see if you can make the picture more or less compelling. Try making it bigger, smaller, brighter, duller, nearer, further away. If your feelings about it change, then these are the critical submodalities.
5. Break state. Do something to take your mind off the picture for a moment.
6. Now imagine the behaviour or habit you do want (desired state). Make this picture compelling so that you really feel motivated to have this in your life.
7. Check the picture is good for you and your life as a whole.
8. Make it dissociated.
9. Break state.
10. Now go back to the original picture, your unwanted behaviour, and *ramp up* the critical submodalities. For example, if size is important, make it very large. If brightness is important, make it very bright. There should be two main submodalities that make the difference. Make sure you are still associated.
11. Take your second picture, the desired state, and shrink it down into a small dissociated picture into the bottom left-hand corner of your vision.
12. *Swish.* As quickly as you can, switch the two pictures. The unwanted behaviour shrinks down into the bottom left-hand corner, becoming a dark dot. The new desired behaviour swishes across becoming big and bright (or gains your two critical submodalities). Make a *swish* sound as you do it.
13. Blank your mind. Break state and look somewhere else for a few seconds.
14. Now repeat the swish.
15. Break state and repeat the swish several times – at least three.
16. Test. You will find that the picture of your old behaviour probably won't be the same any more.
17. Future pace. How are you going to behave in the future? See what picture comes into your head.

Phobias

A phobia is set up when a person has had an extremely intense or unpleasant experience and has anchored the strong negative emotion to something. Next time he comes into contact with that thing, it will trigger the same response. However, because the brain has attached a trigger in this way, it is possible to teach it to produce a positive emotion in place of the phobic response.

How to cure a phobia

This is laid out as if you are doing it with another person. It is best to undertake this with another person so that you can guide him to remain disassociated from the event where needed.

1. First, ask the person to recall his phobia. Make sure that the person only thinks about it very quickly and avoids associating into the emotion. Calibrate any changes in his physiology when he does this. You will be able to compare this with his response after the technique.

2. Break that person's state so he can get out of this physiology.

3. Establish a resource anchor. Ask them to get into a positive state by recalling a time when the person felt a positive emotion in the past. As he does this, anchor it to one of his knuckles by touching it when you observe him reaching the peak of the positive emotion. (You can ensure he can get back a positive emotion any time he needs to by triggering this anchor.)

4. Now ask the person to imagine he is in the projection room of a cinema watching a film in front of him and below him.

must know

Phobias are an example of 'one-trial' learning. With a phobia, you do something once and afterwards you can do it again and again. It is useful to remember (or to remind anyone you are helping) that if the brain can learn to do something this effortlessly, then it can learn to do something more useful just as easily.

5. Ask him to ask his unconscious mind to project the very first intense experience that led to the phobia. (He will come up with something even if he is not certain that it is the earliest event.)

6. Keep the person dissociated from this first event by having him watch a film of himself from just before that first event (when everything was pleasant) to the point afterwards (when everything felt safe again). Make sure he makes the film black and white, as colour can intensify the emotion for some people.

7. Freeze the final frame of the film and white (or black) it out.

8. Break state.

9. Now ask the other person to associate into the end of the film (where it feels safe). Run the whole film back as quickly as possible in colour to the beginning, staying associated.

10. Break state.

11. Repeat that step again (at least three times) until the person can't get the original emotions back. (If you are using this technique for a memory, rather than a phobia, repeat it until the memory can't be accessed.)

12. Check the ecology. Is it OK for the person to have changed this reaction? Will he need to behave differently in the future? Does he need any additional resources? You can do a swish pattern at this point (see page 150). Make sure the person has appropriate responses to his previous phobia – for example, make sure he is still cautious about a dangerous animal.

13. Test and future pace. How does the person feel? When he imagines coming into contact with the object or animal in the future, how does he react?

Erasure

This technique is an adaptation of the phobia cure and can be used for painful past memories.

Erasure technique

This is laid out as if you were doing it for yourself, but you can also do it with another person.

1. Get yourself into a strong, positive state.
2. Create a positive resource anchor (see *Phobias*, pages 151–52.
3. Identify a negative event from your past.
4. Run a film of the event from just before the beginning to just after the end as if it were on a movie screen, so you remain dissociated.
5. Smile and get into a happy state. Run the entire memory backwards as fast as it can go.
6. Now double the speed and run it forwards to the end and stop.
7. Next, run it backwards and forwards repeatedly as quickly as possible. Each time the film will look more and more strange (and it will probably also seem funny).
8. When you next think of the old memory you should feel neutral.

must know

There is no failure, only feedback. Feedback allows you to adapt and change, refocus and increase your chances of success by testing out the possibilities in new situations.

Turning a problem into an opportunity

How do you bring about change? How do you do anything you have never done before? By experimentation and making lots of mistakes.

Successful people use their mistakes in a creative way. They take everything that happens to

must know

'Problem' to 'opportunity'
- elicit
- brainstorm
- logic
- consequences
- ecology
- values
- future pace
- action

them as a process of feedback. Here's how to turn a problem in to an opportunity.

► *Elicit*. Clarify what the 'problem' is. State it in detailed terms.

► *Brainstorm*. List all the possible ways in which you can solve the problem. You should count in any options at this point. Let your unconscious generate as many possibilities as possible. Keep your conscious logical mind out of the picture at this stage.

► *Logic*. Now use your conscious logical mind. For each possibility you have written down, write down the steps that you would need to take to achieve it.

► *Consequences*. Look at the consequences of each option. Ask yourself what would happen if you take those steps.

► *Ecology*. What effect would pursuing each option have on your life?

► *Values*. What values do you have for this part of your life? How does each option fulfil or conflict with your values in this area?

► *Future pace*. What will it feel like, sound like, look like when you take each option? Which option is most appealing to you?

► *Action:* What is the first step you are going to take to achieve your outcome?

Changing values

In Chapter 3 we looked at how to identify your values. A value is what motivates you, or what is important to you – the 'why'. The NLP change values techniques will allow you to change your own or someone else's values.

When to change values

You need to change your values when they are not in alignment with a specific outcome and/or your general purpose in life.

must know

If you set an outcome without aligning your values, you won't reach it because your motivation won't be there.

How to change values

Detailed values elicitation

First you have to find out where you are now (present state). What are your values?

1. What's important to you about...? Pick an area of your life you want to change, for example your career, relationship or money. Write down the answers.

2. Next, put them in order. Number them according to their importance. To do this, ask yourself: 'Which of the above values is the most important to me?' 'If I had value X and not value Y, would that be OK?' 'What if it were the other way around?'

3. Rewrite the list of values according to the importance.

The meaning of the values

▶ What does value X/Y mean to you? Different words mean different things for each person. Asking for the meaning or *complex equivalence* of a word can tweak out deeper values and unconscious beliefs. The meaning you personally give to a word such as challenge or happiness is what's important – not how another person interprets it.

must know

Away from values
will create want
you don't want in
your life.

Towards or away from

▶ Why is that value important to you? Is it something you want to move *towards* or *away from*? If you are primarily motivated by 'stick' rather than 'carrot' your motivation strategy may be uncomfortable at times.

Values conflicts

▶ Are there any conflicts emerging? Check to see whether each value on the list is aligned with the others. Starting with the lowest value, does it support the one above it and does that one support the one above that? If not, you can use the changing values process *(see below)*.

▶ Did your motivation for the values include any words like 'should', 'ought', 'have to' or any *away from* motivations? Check for any limiting beliefs.

▶ Conflict can occur even if you are motivated completely by *towards* values. Do you want two things that you can't achieve at the same time in this particular context, for example total freedom and total security? To resolve conflicting values, use the parts integration technique *(see next page)*.

Threshold values

These are key values. To elicit them, look at your values list for a particular area. Ask yourself: 'If you had all these values present, what would make you leave the situation?' The answer you give is a 'threshold value'. Add it to your list, then ask 'and if this value too is present in the situation what would make you stay'. If you get another answer, add this to your list too.

Changing values technique

To change the position of a value in a hierarchy, use a similar technique to a belief change:

▶ Find out (elicit) the submodalities of the value you wish to replace (A).
▶ Elicit the submodalities of the value you wish to replace it with (B).
▶ Take picture B and change the submodalities to those of picture A.
▶ Elicit the values hierarchy list again and check that B is where you want it to be.

Parts integration

Sometimes there is a conflict between values because one part of you wants one thing and another part wants another. You might even hear yourself using the words, 'one side' or 'on the one hand'. The parts integration technique can be used to resolve this.

Detached parts

The theory is that a 'part' is a part of the unconscious that has become detached from the whole because of a significant emotional event. These parts then cause incongruent behaviour because they each have their own purpose.

For example, if you sometimes move towards making money and sometimes give it all up to create time for yourself, there may be a parts conflict between time and money.

Parts integration technique

▶ Identify the parts. Hold your hands out in front of you and ask the unwanted behaviour or part to come out onto one hand and its opposite to come out on the other.
▶ Get a picture, feeling or sound image for each part.
▶ Ask each part:
  'What is the purpose of [the behaviour]?'
▶ For every word that comes up, repeat the question until you reach a common purpose on each side.
▶ Let the parts notice that they have the same intention and ask what resources each has that the other would like.
▶ Now remind the parts that they were once part of a larger whole.
▶ Bring your hands together and allow the parts to integrate.
▶ Bring the integrated image inside your body by symbolically placing your hands on your chest. You may feel something happen in your body as you do this.
▶ Test and future pace.

9 Discovering your strategies for success

All your everyday behaviour is determined by your strategies. A strategy is the order in which you do things to produce a result. You have different strategies for love, learning, motivation, being convinced and making decisions. This chapter looks at how to discover your strategies in order to produce a new outcome.

Strategies

How aware are you of the strategies you use to decide when to fall in love, what to eat and drink or what to buy? Were you even aware that you had strategies for these things? A strategy is the 'way' you do something – the order and sequence that produces an outcome. When you change a strategy you can produce a different outcome.

Recipes for the brain

Many of the strategies we use to get different results are entirely unconscious. NLP is concerned with how your strategies work, how you can change them to produce different results and how you can master strategies of excellence. How do you make a cake? A strategy is like a recipe for the brain – a set of experiences that take place in a particular order or sequence and lead to a result.

Types of strategy

There are many different types of strategy. Some of the key strategies you may want to discover are your learning, decision-making, motivation, buying, deep love and problem strategies. If these are working well for you, then that's obviously fine. However, there may be some that you wish to change.

Learning strategy
Your learning strategy provides the means by which you pick up and retain new information. You may have different learning strategies for different subjects.

Decision-making strategy
Decision-making strategies govern how you come up with a decision. Some people have decision-making strategies that are so complex that they rarely reach the

point of making a decision. If you belong in this category, you need to examine your strategies.

Motivation strategy

Motivation strategies are the means by which you get yourself to do something. If you don't find it easy to start or complete tasks, take a look at your motivation strategies.

Buying strategy

If you are in business, it is essential to understand your customers' buying strategies. How they make the decision unconsciously may be very different from the reasons they give you out loud.

How do you decide to buy something in your personal life? If you have a large credit bill and a lot of possessions you don't really need, your buying strategy may not be working for you. You need to change it so that you are spending within your means, not following your shopping impulses.

Deep love strategy

Do you know how you know that you are in love with someone or that you are deeply loved by someone? It may be useful to understand your own and your partner's deep love strategy.

Problem strategy

Have you ever met someone who is always complaining about the number of problems that he has. A problem is simply an outcome that a person doesn't want. 'Chunk down' (see pages 118–19). Get specific and identify what results that person is getting that he no longer wants. For each problem, check the strategy – find out how he is producing the result. Once you know the strategy you can change it.

Smoking, drinking, overeating

If you produce a specific action that is a problem for you, for example smoking, eating or drinking too much, you can change your strategies and lose the problem.

must know

Micro-strategies, macro-strategies
Micro-strategies are the sequence of *unconscious* steps that make up a certain way of behaving, for example your strategy for falling in love.
Macro-strategies are the different actions you take unconsciously *and* consciously to get a result.

must know

The make-up of a strategy
Every strategy is made up of a number of representational systems that occur in a particular sequence.
Every representational system is stored in submodalities.
Every strategy leads to an outcome.

Using strategies

If you think about the phrase 'the cat sat on the mat' it has a different meaning from the phrase 'the mat sat on the cat', even though it contains exactly the same words. Order and sequence are important to understanding.

How strategies are stored in the brain

In the same way, your experiences are stored in your brain using the five representational systems (visual, auditory, kinaesthetic, olfactory and gustatory). They are refined by the submodalities in which they are stored. In addition, they are stored with reference to the order in which they occur – a strategy. Every sequence of stored experiences leads to an outcome.

External and internal strategies

You do things externally – behaviour – in an order. You also think internally in an order. The order in which you do things and in which your thoughts occur are both strategies. All your external behaviour is also controlled by an internal strategy.

Change your strategies, change your results

If a strategy is repeated exactly in the way and order it occurs, it will produce the same results. If you change it in any way, either internally or externally, it will produce a different result.

One reason you may want to learn more about your strategies is that if they are not getting you the results you want in your life, you can change them to produce results that suit you better. Another reason to become aware of your strategies is so that you can not just get different results but *truly excellent* results. If you want to learn how to be successful at something, look for a person who is a master at it. Replicate their strategy and you should be able to become a master at it too.

The TOTE model

There are several models you can use to discover your own and other people's strategies. The TOTE model is the most commonly used NLP model for analysing someone's micro (or unconscious) strategies.

Describing a strategy

The TOTE model comes from the work of George Miller, Eugene Galanter and Karl Pribram and was outlined in their book *Plans and the Structure of Behaviour* (see page 186). Every strategy you run can be broken down according to this model. The TOTE model lays out the route between where you are now (the present state) and an end state – how you go from the starting point of not doing something to the place where you do it. Before using the TOTE model, decide what strategy you are looking at. The TOTE model consists of four parts that generally happen very quickly and outside your conscious awareness:

must know

You can change a strategy in order to produce either a different outcome or to install a new strategy.

1. Test (T)

In the first test you compare where you are now (the present state) with where you want to be (your outcome or desired state). If there is a gap between the two, then something needs to happen for you to get what you want. For example, you want to make a decision. The test stage shows that you haven't decided yet.

2. Operate (O)

In order to reach the desired state (in this case a decision), you take an action. This is a data-gathering stage. You might evaluate lots of different data and come up with several actions that you could take.

must know

The process of finding out another person's strategy is called *eliciting a strategy*. There are two ways to elicit a strategy:
1. Ask the person a series of questions *(see below)*.
2. Observe him carrying out a task and note the sequence of their behaviour.

T

TEST
T = Compare current
and desired states

O ⬇

OPERATE
O = Take action,
gather data and
generate alternatives

T ⬇

TEST
T = Check data and
evidence desired state/
outcome has been
achieved

E ⬇

EXIT
E = Exit when criteria
for desired state
achieved

=  **TOTE**

To find out how another person does this stage, ask them questions about what they do, in what order, and if any step doesn't work, what they do next. (The questions to ask are given in detail in *Other people's strategies* on the following pages.)

Some actions are very simple, but others are more complex and may be made up of more than one TOTE. If you have a lot of choice at the operate stage, then you are more likely to be able to move from your present state to your desired state.

3. Test (T)

The second test checks whether you have taken an action or several actions that are sufficient to allow the gap between the present stage and desired state to disappear. For example, have you unconsciously gathered enough information to allow yourself to decide now?

4. Exit (E)

If the answer is 'yes', then the outcome is achieved and the strategy *exits* or completes. In this case, a decision is made. If the answer is 'no', then the strategy can't exit and you find yourself unable to come to a decision.

Other people's strategies

If you are working with another person and need to find out (elicit) their strategies, you can use the following technique.

How to find out another person's strategy

▶ Get into rapport with the other person (see pages 70–71).

▶ Get into the state you want to elicit. Since you are both in rapport, this helps the other person to get into the right state too.

▶ Make sure the other person is associated into the state in the situation you want to ask him about. Calibrate him to make sure the state he is experiencing is intense.

▶ Anchor the state (see pages 130–37).

▶ Fire the anchor.

▶ Ask the person a series of questions to get the sequence of steps in the strategy (the operate part of the TOTE model):

> 'Can you recall a time when you were totally motivated/in love/learning well?'
>
> 'Can you recall a specific time?'
>
> 'As you go back to that time now...what was the very first thing that caused you to be totally motivated/in love/learning well?'
>
> 'Was it something you saw? Was it the way someone looked at you?'
>
> 'Was it something you heard? Was it someone's tone of voice?'
>
> 'Was it the touch of someone or something?'
>
> 'What was the very first thing that caused you to be totally motivated/in love/learning well?'

▶ The person may come up with an answer that is visual, kinaesthetic or auditory. Ask that person for the next step in the sequence.

> 'After you saw/heard/felt that, what was the very next thing that happened?'

'Did you picture something in your mind?'
'Did you say something to yourself?'
'Did you have a certain feeling or emotion?'
'What was the next thing that happened?'
'After you did that, did you know that you were totally motivated/in love/learning well?'
▶ Check you have a logical sequence of steps.
▶ Check that you have the key pieces of the strategy – the beginning, middle and the end.

Eliciting someone's learning strategy

Ask the person to think of a time when he was able to learn something easily and rapidly. Then ask him:
Test: 'How do you know it is time to begin learning?'
Operation: 'What do you do in order to learn?'
Test: 'How do you know if you have learned something?'
Exit: 'What lets you know that you have learned something fully?'

Eliciting someone's love strategy

If you want to make your relationship secure, make sure you satisfy your partner's love strategy as well as your own. To elicit someone's love strategy ask that person:

'How do you know you are totally loved by someone else?'
'Can you remember a specific time when you were totally loved?'
'In order to know you are totally loved, is it necessary for you:
    to be taken to places and bought things?
    to be looked at with that special look?
    to hear that special tone of voice or those special words?
    to be touched in a certain way or a certain place?'
Check the main representational systems they use and note the order of the strategy.

Writing down a strategy

It is useful to write down a strategy, just like a recipe, so that you can refer back to it when you need to use it again or to modify it in some way.

Note the representational systems

The strategies in NLP are often written down as abbreviations. The abbreviations note not only what representational system is being used at each stage of the strategy but also whether they are *remembered* versus *constructed* (^{r} and ^{c}), and *external* versus *internal* (^{e} and ^{i}).

For example, something you hear inside your head would be written A^i. If you hear someone say something it would be written A^d. If you hear a sound other than words it would be written A^e. Self-talk, or auditory dialogue, is written A^{id}.

If you remember an image you would write V^r. A constructed feeling would be K^c. All strategies exit with an internal feeling: K^i.

An example of a buying strategy

A man sees a shirt in a shop and thinks to himself, 'That looks interesting.' He touches the shirt to feel the texture, then asks the shop assistant the price and decides to buy it. He exits with a good feeling.

This strategy would be written as:

V^e (visual external)

A^{id} (auditory internal digital)

K^e (kinaesthetic external)

A^e (auditory external)

K^i (kinaesthetic internal)

Replacing a strategy

What happens if your strategy doesn't work for you? You can simply design a new one in its place. A simple way of doing this is given on the previous page with the spelling strategy. But what about a more complicated strategy? For example, suppose you want to make quicker decisions?

A simple way of doing this is given on the previous page with the spelling strategy.

must know

Replacing strategies
1. Follow the rules for well-formed strategies to design a new strategy.
2. Install it.

The rules for well-formed strategies

❑ Get clear on the outcome of the strategy. Make sure your representation is well defined, otherwise you won't know how to exit the strategy.

❑ Use all three of the main representational systems (visual, auditory and kinaesthetic).

❑ Make sure the strategy moves towards a decision point (for example, to buy or not to buy something) and doesn't loop back before that point. (For example, if you want to put in an external feeling before you decide to buy something, it will be better to design the strategy so that you only have to do this once or twice. If you make the strategy too complicated, you will never exit it and remain unable to make a decision about whether or not to buy.)

❑ Make sure there is an external check after a certain number of steps. Having external and internal elements to a strategy keeps you from making too many false presuppositions about the external world.

❑ Use only a few steps to get to the outcome you have defined.

❑ Make sure the sequence of steps that you have established is logical.

Installing a strategy

You can install a new strategy in another person by either anchoring it or rehearsing it (*see below*). You can use one of these techniques individually or combine them together, starting with rehearsal then moving on to anchoring.

Rehearsing a strategy

You can run the other person through a new strategy by guiding their eye accessing cues. Point to the appropriate direction for each step with a finger. I.e. to get them to access kinaesthetic, direct them to move their eyes down to the right.

You can also just talk them through the new strategy so that they mentally rehearse it in their minds and see themselves doing it now (associated) and in the future.

Anchoring a strategy

To install a strategy with another person, you can use the chaining anchors technique to chain each step of the new strategy to the next. Anchor each step in turn, for example, using a spatial anchor – ask the person to move to a different position on the floor for each step. Then walk them through the whole sequence and repeat this several times Finally, test the strategy e.g. 'how do you know it's time to buy?' Watch their eye movements (VAK etc) to check that they are doing the new strategy.

watch out!

All strategies should conform to the TOTE model.

10 Using metaphors for success

A metaphor in NLP is any story used to illustrate a point or idea. Storytelling is an age-old tool used to connect with both the conscious and the unconscious and impart wisdom. The listener identifies with a key character in the story and this helps them to accept the message of the story. You can use metaphors to increase the effectiveness of your communication with other people.

Metaphors

Metaphors are another way you can communicate directly with another person's unconscious mind. Stories are easy to remember, while facts and explanations may cause your mind to wander from the subject.

Communicating with metaphors

Metaphors can communicate ideas and information in a situation where if you were to speak about those ideas directly, the listener might be consciously resistant. Metaphors can highlight hopes, beliefs, anxieties and solutions.

The farmer's tale

Once upon a time there was an old man who owned a brown horse that he used to till the earth on his farm so that he could plant corn. One day the horse jumped over the old wooden fence and ran away. The farmer's neighbours came to commiserate. 'What will you do?' they said. 'Without the horse your farm will be ruined!' The farmer simply said, 'Perhaps.'

A few days later the brown horse trotted up to the farm with two white horses. 'You are a lucky man!' the neighbours exclaimed. 'Now you have three horses.' 'Perhaps,' said the farmer.

The next day the farmer's son jumped onto the back of one of the white horses. However, the horse was wild and threw him off. The son broke his leg. 'How unlucky you are,' said the neighbours. 'Perhaps,' said the farmer.

A few days later, a group of soldiers came to press gang every man in the village to go and fight a war. Young man after young man was rounded up, but the farmer's son was allowed to stay in the village. The soldiers didn't want a boy with a broken leg. The neighbours came again and told the farmer how lucky he was. 'Perhaps,' he said...

From fairy stories to films

Metaphors have been used for as long as communication has been recorded. The great philosophers and teachers all used stories in order to simplify the ideas they were teaching.

In Western culture, fairy stories are metaphors that are often used to demonstrate a point about change and transition. Think about stories such as *Cinderella* or *The Ugly Duckling*. How many years have you remembered those stories? It does not matter that they are about a fantasy character, we still identify with their transformation.

Films too can act as metaphors. Experiments have shown that people who are depressed can be helped to feel happier by watching a comedy film or a film with an uplifting message at the end. In any story that has a universal theme, we relate to the central character and the challenges they face and our unconscious draws inspiration for the changes we are facing.

must know

Pick a story based on a hobby or interest that you know the other person is interested in, or a subject that is universal, like cars for example. That way you will keep the attention of your audience because they become emotionally involved in the outcome of the story.

How to use metaphors

1. Choose a metaphor that your listener can relate to and that is appropriate in the context you are using it.
2. Use the metaphor to establish rapport. Storytelling is fun.
3. Relate each feature of the idea you are selling to a feature in the story.
4. Use language of the representational system that your listener will most relate to.
5. Keep the language positive. Always create a positive internal representation inside the listener's head as you move him within the story to your goal. Avoid clichés.
6. You can also use embedded quotes. Have one person say something to another in the story in quotes, for example, 'Just pay attention to what I have to say.' The listener will feel that he is being addressed directly without finding the statement confrontational.
7. If you think the listener has a question about the idea that you are expressing, actually state that question in the story (perhaps as if it is said by a character) and then answer it in the story as well.

Using metaphors

The best stories will capture the imagination and provoke the listener to look at a situation afresh or to do something that he might not otherwise have attempted. A metaphor is also a wonderful way to bypass the conscious mind and to help another person to come up with their own solutions for change.

What does it mean for you?

Metaphors can seem at first to be stories with no relevance to anything you want to achieve for yourself. Then, after a while, you realize that all the characters and images and words are starting to mean something to you.

Even if you don't realize that straightaway, your unconscious enjoys working out what the story might mean for you, and that in itself can bring new realizations.

How a metaphor is heard

Metaphors engage the right brain in the same way as dreams, because they are symbolic and entertain as well as inform. The listener takes from the metaphor what he wants to take unconsciously and applies it to his own situation. Resistance to accepting the message is decreased because a story is much less confrontational than a direct statement addressed to the conscious mind. Within the content of the story you can present different points of view, suggest actions and propose solutions.

As the story is a flexible format, many states can be elicited during the course of the metaphor. It provides sufficient scope to reframe the listener and

did you know?

In business, great motivational speakers use metaphors to put across their points and displace resistance to their ideas. If you are using a metaphor in a business situation, make your stories relevant. Choose a story about a business that was successful, or choose a common analogy that is used in business such as battling the opposition or racing ahead of the competition. Tell a story about a battle or a race, and make sure that it has the ending that fits the scenario you want to lay forth.

take him from a negative state to an intermediate state to a positive state. In a longer metaphor, you could take someone from a state of not making a decision to becoming interested, to seeing several different possibilities and then deciding on one. Just think how useful that would be with a person who does not find it easy to make up his mind or gets stuck in one state and finds it impossible to move on.

Metaphors from personal experience

Fairy tales and films are examples of metaphors that draw on archetypal images. The second type of metaphor is personal and was described by the therapist David Grove, who studied NLP and Ericksonian hypnosis and worked with traumatic memories and phobias. His work has been extensively modelled and developed by Penny Tomkins and James Lawley.

You can work out what these personal metaphors are by listening to what a person says. They may just be a turn of phrase, an expression, an image that keeps coming to mind or even a memory, it doesn't matter. They describe a real experience that the person has internally. The metaphor shows *how* he has stored this experience in sensory terms, whether it is visual, auditory, kinaesthetic, gustatory or olfactory.

Personal metaphors contain lots of valuable information about how the person perceives and thinks about the world. This information is revealed in symbolic form in the words he uses. Any metaphor you hear a person use has a special significance for him.

must know

The brain has two different hemispheres. The left brain is the logical side. It is objective and analytical and processes data sequentially. The right brain uses language of images and symbols. It notices our non-verbal language and processes information simultaneously.

must know

Key questions
'What's that like to you?'
'What kind of [metaphor] is that?'
'Is there anything else?'

watch out!

When you are getting information from another person about his metaphors, make sure you use 'clean language' – that is, you use his own words and don't add your own information. If the other person repeats the question you have asked, it's an indication that it may not be the best question.

Listen for both overt and implied metaphors in a person's speech: 'I am feeling under pressure' is an implied metaphor, as is 'I need space' or 'I feel down at the moment'.

Using metaphors to uncover meaning

Personal metaphors can explain a lot. Suppose you are discussing a difficulty a person is having and he says, 'I feel a knot in my stomach every time I get anxious.' You can uncover the personal *significance*, *function* and *attributes* the person has given to this knot – what it means to them.

Attributes of personal metaphor

Using the other person's language, ask that person for further details about the metaphor. Get him to describe it:

▶ What exactly does it look like? How big is it? How thick is it? What is it made out of? Attributes can show you the function of the metaphor.

▶ Location: Where is it? What direction is it in? Symbols are stored in precise locations.

▶ Time and sequence. See if there is a sequence of events in the description of the metaphor. The order of events in a person's internal metaphorical landscape is important.

Suppose the person answers: 'The knot is brown with black bits, quite large, as if it has taken over my whole stomach.' Straightaway you have more words and images to work with. 'Taken over?' 'What's that like to you?'

Is it a knot that is hard or one that is soft and pliable? One person might see the knot as acting like a shield, while another person sees it as preventing some action and yet another as absorbing an emotion.

Overt or implied

A person may use metaphors that are overt or implied. Some examples:

Overt metaphors

'I keep hitting my head against a brick wall.'

'He broke my heart.'

'You look a bit down in the dumps.'

'My parents really get under my skin.'

Implied metaphors

'Stop running away from the argument.'

'I am feeling under enormous pressure here.'

'I feel I can't get through to him any more.'

'I need to get some distance from this problem.'

The story of the wisest man

A king once wanted to find the wisest man in the kingdom to be his prime minister. When he asked his courtiers for help in finding the ideal candidate, they said there were three men in the kingdom who were wiser than all the others.

The king called all three men to his palace and set them a test. He shut them all in the same room and told them that they had been locked in with the most complex lock ever devised. He said that whoever could open the lock first would be appointed the head of his government.

Two of the wise men immediately began to calculate the combination of the lock using the most advanced mathematics. They scribbled and added up and multiplied and reasoned frantically.

Meanwhile, the third wise man sat and did nothing but think quietly. Then, after a little while, he walked over to the door and put his hand on the handle. The unlocked door opened immediately...

11 Putting it all together

How do you use NLP in a systematic way to
create better results in your personal life, in
business or to help other people around you?
This chapter looks at ways in which you can
bring together the techniques of NLP to
create better results.

Applications of NLP

You can use NLP in your personal life, you can use it to help or coach another person or you can apply it in a business situation.Because NLP is about modelling excellence, you can use it in any situation where you want to learn how someone does something well.

When to use different NLP techniques

Here are some of the situations in which you can use specific techniques:

▶ *Anchors:* to move from a negative state to a positive state, including depression (stacking and chaining anchors as well as resource anchoring)

▶ *Association:* to have (or get someone to have) a 'real' experience of something

▶ *Belief change:* to resolve an unconscious conflict that is stopping the achievement of an outcome in any area; to deal with fears and limits

▶ *Disney strategy:* to produce creative thinking and an achievable vision

▶ *Dissociation:* to get rid of over-involvement

▶ *Logical levels:* to check the alignment of change throughout all neurological levels

▶ *Matching and mirroring:* to gain rapport in personal or business relationships, particularly in presentations, meetings, negotiation and selling

▶ *Meta Model:* to challenge thinking and move from a state of 'stuckness'

▶ *Metaphors:* to loosen up thinking and produce a new state or unconscious change

▶ *Mental rehearsal:* to future pace a situation to create change or to see how effective change has been

▶ *Milton Model:* to create trance

▶ *Outcomes:* to get clear on aims and how to achieve them

▶ *Parts integration:* to address self-sabotage situations and conflicts in outcomes

▶ *Pattern interrupt:* to change state

▶ *Perceptual positions:* to change a viewpoint about a relationship

▶ *Phobia process:* to resolve phobias and traumas

▶ *Rapport:* when using techniques with others

▶ *Reframing:* to change an outlook or viewpoint

▶ *Six-step reframe:* to address self-sabotage situations; to change habits

▶ *Swish pattern:* to change a habit

▶ *Values alignment:* to resolve an unconscious conflict that is blocking an outcome

Using NLP techniques for yourself

When you want a new result, remember to start by getting clear about where you are now (your present state). Clarify your values and beliefs. Then write down an outcome (your desired state). Now identify what depth of change is needed for you to move from your present state to your desired state.

Change on many levels

NLP techniques can be used to produce change on many different levels. On a basic level, you can use simple techniques such as reframing, perceptual positions and future pacing to shake up your thinking and see a situation differently. Anchoring too, will result in a quick change by producing more resourceful states. If you want to stop biting your nails or eat less chocolate, this may just be a matter of using a swish pattern and the habit will change straightaway. However, often the issues we want to resolve, or the outcomes we want, are not achievable by just one technique. For example, to resolve low self-esteem, forge better relationships, lose weight or discover why you keep creating situations in which you get into debt, you need to discover what is going on beneath the surface and to use a combination of some of the deeper techniques. These include values and belief changes, strategies, metaphors and six-step reframes.

Finally, you may want to gain new resources and/or learn a new skill. If so, the quickest way to produce change may be to find a model of excellence and learn his strategies for success.

must know

In NLP, a simple one-outcome change is known as *first order change*. A change that affects not just the original issue but is also generative and creates new ways of thinking is known as *second order change*.

The modelling process

When you model someone else you work out how that person does what he does well and how you can replicate it. You might want to model how another person has good relationships, makes money or sells successfully, or how he drives or plays a sport well. In fact, you can model any strategy.

must know

Remember that the modelling is the process by which you discover how someone gets from the starting point of not doing, having or being something (present state) to doing, having or being something (desired state).

How to model someone

▶ First identify a person who is really excellent at what he does. Obviously, find the best person to model, otherwise you will simply adopt the flaws in the behaviour you are modelling.

▶ If you are talking about a large subject, for example running a successful business, it may be useful to break what the person does into small chunks or components, for example how the firm sells, manages people, maintains client relationships, etc. It may be useful to start with the smallest and easiest component.

The essential ingredients to modelling

▶ *What is going on physically in the person's body?* Observe that person's physiology. How does he stand, sit or move? Particularly pay attention to his posture and the angle of his spine as well as his breathing.

▶ *Why does that person do what he does?* What provides the motivation for the consistent results that the person gets? What are his filter patterns? If you can ask him directly, do so. Otherwise, work them out by observing the person's behaviour and listening to what he says. What are his meta programmes, values and core beliefs with regard to what you want to model? Why does he behave in the way that he does?

▶ *Strategies* Observe the strategies that person uses such as the order and sequence in which he does things, or elicit his internal strategies (see pages 160–61) to find out what is going on outside his conscious awareness to produce his behaviour.

▶ *Feedback* Pay attention to how that person gets feedback on his progress and success.

▶ *What is critical?* Find out what is essential to obtaining the end result, rather than what is simply unique to that person.

▶ *Test* Write down what you observe and test out your theory by dropping different elements until you determine what is essential and what is not.

▶ *Do it yourself* What happens when you adopt the same ways of thinking, do things for the same reason and replicate the actions they take? If you don't get the same results consistently, what have you missed?

▶ *Teach someone else* If you do get the same results consistently, you should be able to show someone else how to get them as well. Now you have successfully modelled a strategy for success.

Modelling yourself

What if you sometimes do things very well yourself, but are not consistent? You can model your own behaviour too.

1. Identify what it is you want to do well. Pay attention to why you want to do it. What are your values? How about your beliefs and meta programmes? What strategies do you use?

2. What is the difference that makes a difference? Discover what is essential to reproducing the behaviour and what is not.

3. Decide on what you think is the pattern of actions, beliefs, values, etc., and the order and sequence in which you use them to get the desired result.

4. Test your theories by missing out pieces of the pattern, then consciously start dropping pieces to find what is essential.

Using NLP techniques with others

When you are coaching another person, make sure that he takes responsibility for the results he gets. How motivated is *he* to change? It is that person, not you, who will be making the changes. You are simply giving him the techniques to do so.

Working with other people

Before coaching another person, do remind him of the cause/effect equation. For every effect there is a cause. So he has created the results that he has in his life right now. He is responsible for his future results too. Not you.

Also introduce the person to the core beliefs or presuppositions of NLP, especially 'People already have all the resources they need.' Make it clear that you are not a therapist or a doctor. You can simply help someone to discover and use his own resources through the NLP techniques.

As you use the NLP techniques with other people, keep in mind the idea of 'experimentation'. Have fun and try things. Be flexible and you will get the result you want.

How to use the NLP techniques to create an outcome

▶ *Check your state and your congruency:* Whenever you use NLP techniques with another person, make sure that you are in a positive state and believe that you and the other person are able to get the positive result that they want.

▶ *Get rapport:* Use the rapport-building skills that have been outlined in *Forming Relationships* (see pages 67–77), for example calibration, matching and mirroring.

▶ *What is that person's outcome?* Why is he here? What is the issue he wants to resolve? What is the result he is getting? What does he want instead? Introduce the person to the beliefs of NLP.

▶ *Map his existing model of the world:* Use the Meta Model to gather information about his model of the world. Notice the representational systems he uses, his meta programmes, beliefs and values.

▶ *What needs to change?* Notice what resources the person has already to get his outcome. What limits him? What needs to change? Pay attention to any belief or value conflicts and strategies that are not effective. Pay attention to any core issues relating to his outcome – what is the difference that will make the most difference?

▶ *Loosen his model of the world:* Use the Milton Model, Meta Model, chunking, perceptual positions and reframing to show the person what he has deleted, distorted, generalized and filtered.

▶ *Create change and build resources:* Depending on the situation, you may want to use just one technique or several. How can you help the person to resolve any conflicts, remove blocks and build his existing resources? Use anchoring, reframing, swish patterns, belief and values changes or strategy changes. Check for alignment with the Logical Levels model.

▶ *Test the result:* Check whether or not the techniques you have used have been successful. Observe (calibrate for) changes in his language and physiology. Elicit beliefs and values to check how the person has changed. Notice if there has been any change in his representational system. If there are any incongruencies, you may need to use the parts integration technique.

▶ *Future pace:* Check that the result will be ongoing. What new behaviour will the person be exhibiting? The simplest way to do this is to get him to imagine himself at a specific time in the future. Use associated and dissociated mental rehearsal. A three-month time frame works well enough to convince many people, though you may want to go much further if he is very big picture in his thinking or to ask him to imagine several points in the future. When he is there, ask him what he sees, hears and feels. Is he on the way to achieving the result he asked for?

Further reading

Books

Harry Adler, *NLP: The New Art and Science of Getting What You Want*, Piatkus Books 1994

Steve and Connirae Andreas, *Change Your Mind and Keep the Change*, Real People Press 1988

Steve and Connirae Andreas, *Core Transformation*, Real People Press 1996

Steve Andreas and Charles Faulkner, *NLP: The Technology of Achievement*, Nicholas Brealey Publishing Ltd 1996

Richard Bandler, *Using Your Brain for a Change*, Real People Press 1985

Richard Bandler and John Grinder, *Frogs into Princes*, Real People Press 1981

Richard Bandler and John Grinder, *The Structure of Magic: A Book About Language and Therapy*, v. I, Science and Behaviour Books 1989

Michael Brooks, *Instant Rapport*, Time Warner International 1990

Robert Dilts, *Changing Belief Systems with NLP*, Meta Publications, 1990

Robert Dilts, *Visionary Leadership Skills*, Meta Publications, 1996

Robert Dilts, Tim Hallborn and Suzie Smith, *Beliefs*, Metamorphous Press 1990

Christopher Howard, *Turning Passions into Profit: Three Steps to Wealth and Power*, John Wiley 2005

David Gordon, *Therapeutic Metaphors: Helping Others Through the Looking Glass*, Gordon Meta Publications 1989

Sue Knight, *NLP at Work: The Difference that Makes a Difference in Business*, Nicholas Brealey Publishing Ltd 2002

Tad James and Wyatt Woodsmall, *Time Line Therapy and the Basis of Personality*, Meta Publications 1989

Michael McMaster and John Grinder, *Precision: New Approach to Communication*, Metamorphous Press 1994

George Miller, Eugene Galanter and Karl Pribam, *Plans and the Structure of Behaviour*, Holt, R&W 1969

Joseph O'Connor and John Seymour, *Introducing NLP*, HarperCollins 2003

John Overdurf and Julie Silverthorn, *Training Trances*, Metamorphous Press 1995

Anthony Robbins, *Unlimited Power*, Pocket Books 2001

Anthony Robbins, *Awaken the Giant Within*, Pocket Books 1993

Michael Talbot, *The Holographic Universe*, HarperCollins 1996

David Shepherd and Tad James, *Presenting Magically: Transforming Your Stage Presence with NLP*, Crown House Publishing 2001

---

want to know more?

Websites

http://www.nlpuniversitypress.com/indexR.html Online NLP encyclopedia

http://www.cleanlanguage.co.uk/ Symbolic modelling, clean language, the metaphor therapy of David Grove

www.davidgrove.com The metaphor therapy of David Grove

Glossary

Accessing cues The movements that show how a person is thinking and processing information inside themselves. They include eye movements, gestures, breathing and changes in posture.

Align To co-ordinate or arrange so that all steps and parts of a process are moving towards the same outcome.

Anchor An external stimulus or trigger that sets off an internal response. Can be visual, auditory or kinaesthetic.

As if frame Imagining an experience in the future as if it has already happened.

Behavioural flexibility Having the ability to change your ways of doing things and being around other people in order to get the outcome or response you want from them.

Break state Doing something that quickly changes the focus of your attention and your state.

Calibration/to calibrate The ability to observe what is going on with another person through reading their non-verbal signals.

Chaining anchors Changing someone's emotional state by setting up a series of anchors that they move through one by one to move from the present state to a desired state.

Chunking Gaining a different viewpoint by looking at a situation from a different level. To chunk, you can move up, down or sideways.

Congruence When your outcome is fully aligned with your beliefs, values, identity, etc. and when your verbal communication is aligned with your non-verbal communication.

Context reframe Giving a new perspective and meaning to something by changing the context.

Deep structure What lies beneath surface language and behaviour.

Dissociated A state of being outside an experience rather than looking at it through your own eyes.

Distortion An internal representation that is changed in some way.

Down time Being focused on your own experience.

Ecology Paying attention to the relationship between yourself and your environment. Internal ecology looks at the congruency of a person's values and behaviour and outcomes.

Elicitation Finding out the necessary information to determine behaviour or strategy.

Eye movements/accessing cues Changes in the directions in which the eyes move when thinking in the visual, auditory and kinaesthetic systems and imagining or remembering.

First position Looking at the world from your own point of view.

Frame A particular way of looking at something. By changing the frame you can change the meaning.

Future pacing Mentally rehearsing/trying on an experience in the future as if it is happening to you now in order to get the desired behaviour to occur naturally and unconsciously.

Generalization The process by which one part of your experience is changed to become a class of experience.

Incongruence Lack of congruence and alignment leading to blocks and internal conflict in realizing an outcome.

Intention The conscious or unconscious purpose of behaviour.

Internal representation How you store information in your mind in terms of pictures, sounds, tastes, smells and feelings – sensory modalities.

Lead representational system The system you use to access your internal information.

Leading Keeping rapport with another person while changing your behaviour or body movements so

Glossary

that they follow you. The unconscious leader of a group is known as a rapport leader.

Logical levels *See* Neurological levels.

Map 'The map is not the territory' – the unique world you have created out of your experience.

Meta Model A set of questions and language patterns designed to uncover deletion, generalization and distortion and to give additional resources.

Meta programme The unconscious programming we all have on a mental level that decides how we filter and chunk experience.

Milton Model The model of language patterns based on the speech and techniques of hypnotherapist Milton Erickson. It uses deliberately vague language to communicate with the unconscious.

Modal operators Language patterns to do with possibility or necessity, for example 'may', 'can'.

Modelling Analyzing how something works systematically and breaking it down into a usable model that can be replicated by other people to achieve a desired outcome.

Neurological Relating to the nervous system.

Neurological change Change at a physical and mental level.

Neurological levels A model of environment, behaviour, capability, belief, identity and spirituality.

Outcome A goal, result or desired state that has been defined in specific terms to do with seeing, feeling or hearing.

Pacing Matching another person's behaviour and thinking to achieve or maintain rapport.

Pattern interrupt Breaking someone's state deliberately and suddenly to interrupt a pattern of behaviour.

Predicate A word that indicates that a person is relating to a particular representational system.

Preferred representational system The representational system a person uses as a matter of preference.

Presuppositions The core beliefs that NLP has adopted as useful beliefs.

Rapport A state in which two people feel a sense of trust and relationship with one another.

Reframing Putting a different frame on an experience in order to give it a positive meaning.

Second position Experiencing the viewpoint of a person other than yourself.

Secondary gain Where behaviour that appears to be negative is providing a benefit that you are not necessarily aware of.

Sensory acuity The process of making very detailed observations of what is going on in terms of visual, auditory, kinaesthetic, olfactory and gustatory data.

Sensory-based description Describing something or someone in terms of verifiable sensory information. Avoids mind reading.

Strategy A sequence of thoughts that leads to an outcome.

Submodalities The small distinctions in how a particular sensory experience is coded internally, for example a picture can be bright or dark.

Surface structure The words or language that show on the surface after the process of deletion, generalization and distortion has changed the deep structure.

Swish pattern A generative technique for changing habits or limiting behaviour.

Territory What is different from the map – the world as it is rather than our own stored experience of it.

Third position Experiencing a situation from the perspective of a person outside the situation.

TOTE Test, Operate, Test, Exit – the sequence that describes the structure of a strategy. The basis for producing any behaviour.

Trance A state of relaxation in which communication with the unconscious is facilitated.

Values hierarchy The order of what is important to you.

Well-formedness conditions The rules for making an outcome specific, sensory-based and achievable.

Index

Index

Index